Boeing Stratoc
and 707

KEY
Books

HISTORIC COMMERCIAL AIRCRAFT SERIES, VOLUME 12

Published by Key Books
An imprint of Key Publishing Ltd
PO Box 100
Stamford
Lincs PE9 1XQ

www.keypublishing.com

Original edition published as *Aeroplane Classic Airliner: Boeing Stratocruiser and 707* © 2013, edited by François Prins

This edition © 2022

All images are from the *Aeroplane* Archive and the Boeing Company, unless otherwise credited.

ISBN 978 1 80282 460 5

Typeset by SJmagic DESIGN SERVICES, India.

Contents

Introduction

William Boeing became interested in aircraft after seeing early examples at an event in California. He established his business and successfully sold aircraft to the United States Armed Forces, as well as forming an air transport operation, which used aircraft of his own making. This led other airlines to buy Boeing aircraft, and, in the years before World War Two, Boeing produced some advanced designs, which included a pressurized airliner and a large, long-range flying boat. The outbreak of war meant that air travel was seriously restricted and future designs were, naturally, placed on hold. Boeing forged ahead with its famous B-17 Flying Fortress bomber,

of which nearly 13,000 had been built by the time the war ended. It also produced the pressurized B-29 Superfortress, which has gone down in history as the aircraft that dropped the atomic bombs on Hiroshima and Nagasaki to end World War Two.

While Boeing was making bombers, Douglas and Lockheed had produced troop transports that were easily adapted as airliners for the postwar market. Boeing produced the Stratocruiser, but it was not a success, and it left the Seattle company looking for an alternative. It was busy with the United States Air Force (USAF) jet bomber program and, using that experience, was able to design and introduce what became the world's most famous airliner in the form of the Boeing 707. For a company that was not known as a commercial aircraft manufacturer, it simply took over the market and dominated the airline scene, which it compounded with the Boeing 747 Jumbo Jet.

Boeing's dominance has recently been challenged by Airbus, with its range of airliners, but Boeing still has a healthy share of the commercial airliner market and looks set to continue to be part of the scene for many years to some.

Chapter 1
The Boeing Company

Born in Detroit in 1881, William Boeing attended Yale University, where he studied engineering. In 1903, Boeing left Yale and headed northwest for Grays Harbor in Washington. Here, he was successful in the timber industry and went on to greater success in Seattle in 1908, where he was involved in a variety of business ventures related to the timber industry. He bought large tracts of woodland, which would stand him in good stead in later years. Boeing also bought and operated a furniture factory and a boatyard, both of which used timber from his own forests. Two years later, Boeing went to Los Angeles, California, to attend the first American air meet. He was impressed by what he saw and tried to obtain a flight in an airplane, but not one of the dozen aviators participating in the event would oblige. Disappointed, Boeing headed back to Seattle but was determined to learn more about aviation.

For the next five years, Boeing explored the theory of aviation in conversation at Seattle's University Club with George Conrad Westervelt, a Navy engineer who had taken several aeronautics courses from the Massachusetts Institute of Technology. The two men looked at as many examples of aircraft as they could and made a flight aboard an early Curtiss-designed biplane, which impressed neither man. Westervelt later wrote that he "could never find any definite answer as to why it held together." Both were convinced they could build a biplane better than any then on the market.

Opposite: **A flying replica of the Boeing Model 1; the original was designed by Conrad Westervelt and flown in 1916.**

Right: **William Boeing (1881–1956) founded the company but left the board in 1934. (Photo: Boeing)**

First Model

In the autumn of 1915, Boeing returned to California to take flying lessons from aviation pioneer Glenn Martin. Before leaving Seattle, Boeing asked Westervelt to start designing a new, more practical aircraft. Construction of the twin-float seaplane began in Boeing's Lake Union boathouse, and was named the B & W, after their initials, but known as the Boeing Model 1. To gain experience, Boeing purchased a Martin floatplane on which he could practice flying off water.

Conrad Westervelt was posted east before the aircraft was finished, so William Boeing continued the project and, in 1916, completed two examples. When it was time for the B & W's first flight on June 15, 1916, the pilot hired was late in arriving. Boeing grew impatient and took the controls himself. As the pilot rushed to the hangar, he saw Boeing taxi to the end of the lake, turn, increase power and take-off for a quarter-mile hop. The 125hp Hall-Scott A-5 engine was more than capable, and the flight was a success.

On July 15, 1916, Boeing incorporated his aircraft manufacturing business as Pacific Aero Products Co.; a year later, he changed the name to the Boeing Airplane Company.

Boeing retained Wong Tsoo, one of the few aeronautical engineers in the country, to design new aircraft for the Seattle enterprise and paid for a wind tunnel at the University of Washington (UW), so the school could offer courses in aeronautics. He also hired Claire Egtvedt and Phil Johnson, both UW engineering scholars, each of whom would later become president of the company.

In 1917, the 28-person Boeing payroll also included pilots, carpenters, boat builders and seamstresses. The lowest wage was 14 cents an hour, while the company's top pilots made US$200 to $300 a month. When the B & W did not sell, Boeing used his own financial resources to guarantee a loan to cover all wages, a total of about $700 a week.

By the end of 1917, the United States had entered World War One, and for the first time, American aircraft were going into battle. Boeing knew the Navy needed training aircraft, and Wong had already designed the Model C seaplane, which was a suitable candidate. However, the small seaplane could not fly all the way from Seattle to the Navy base at Pensacola, Florida, where Navy officials were deciding what to buy.

Undaunted, Boeing had two Model Cs dismantled, packed in crates, and shipped by train across the country. Boeing factory superintendent Claude Berlin and test pilot Herb Munter reassembled the aircraft and flew them for Navy officials. The seaplanes performed well, and the Navy ordered 50 Model Cs; the company's first production order. By May of 1918, 337 people were on the Boeing payroll. Business continued to expand as the military purchased more aircraft for the war effort, but the situation changed when the Armistice came on November 11, 1918; there was no requirement for military aircraft, and the civilian market was equally depressed. William Boeing found he was competing with the mass of war-surplus biplanes that flooded the market. Struggling to survive, the company shed most of its employees and turned its woodworking skills to build dressers, counters and furniture for a corset company and a confectioner's shop, as well as flat-bottomed boats called sea sleds.

Workers steady the Boeing Model 1 as it slides down the slipway at William Boeing's Lake Union boathouse in 1916.

Boeing F4B fighters served with the US Navy in various guises in the interwar years.

The Model 40 could carry 500lb of mail and two passengers and was operated by Boeing Air Transport.

Return to Aircraft

Matters improved in 1920 when Boeing was contracted to convert 300 British-built de Havilland DH.4 aircraft as trainers for the US Army. The Army also ordered 200 Thomas Morse MB-3 fighter aircraft to be license-built by Boeing. This order, together with another later in the year, helped to stabilize the company, which was then able to develop a model that would appeal to the sportsmen who used the many lakes and rivers in Washington state. William Boeing set out to produce a series of small commercial flying boats and floatplanes; only the Model 5 variant sold in any quantity, others remained as prototypes with a single example being manufactured. While sales may have been disappointing, the US Army Air Service (USAAS, the Air Corps [USAAC] after 1926) had recovered from lack of funding following the end of World War One and was starting to expand. Boeing was quick to seize the opportunity and design its Model 15 for the military. Given the official designation PW-9C, the biplane fighter first flew on June 2, 1923, and was ordered into production for the USAAS; the US Navy was also attracted by the PW-9C and ordered some for the Marine Corps, with the designation FB-1. Boeing would continue to develop the single-seat PW/FB series throughout the 1920s and evolve the biplane design into the monoplane fighters that were in service at the end of the 1930s.

To cover the vast continent that is North America, the US Post Office issued contracts for aircraft and pilots to operate an air mail service. With his aircraft business now financially secure, Boeing looked at the air mail operation and concluded that if mail could be carried, so too could passengers. When bidding for the Chicago to San Francisco route was announced, with a start of July 1927, Boeing put in for the contract. For the purpose of winning the contract, Boeing built the Model 40, a landplane capable of carrying 1,000lb of mail plus two passengers in an enclosed cabin. The pilot sat in an exposed cockpit aft of the wings. Boeing won the contract, and the two-dozen aircraft stipulated by the US Post Office were manufactured and tested in time for the July start.

Powered by a single Pratt & Whitney 525hp Hornet radial engine, the Model 40 could carry 500lb of mail plus the passengers at 125mph, with stops at Salt Lake City, Utah, and Omaha, Nebraska.

A new airline, Boeing Air Transport, was created to operate the service and a school to train pilots and engineers was established at Oakland, California. In the first year of operation, Boeing flew

Clyde Pangborn and Roscoe Turner came third in the 1934 MacRobertson Race to Australia flying this Boeing 247 (NR257Y).

some 2,000 passengers and mail aboard the Model 40s with no mishaps or problems. As Boeing Air Transport grew, so too did the need for a larger airliner, and, in July 1928, the company unveiled its twin-engined Model 80, which carried 12 passengers in a comfortable cabin. Unlike the cramped unheated two-place cabin of the Model 40, the new aircraft had heating, reading lamps, leather upholstered seats, and hot and cold running water; the pilots were also brought in from the open cockpit into an enclosed flight deck. Airliners were changing fast to cater for the increasing number of travelers who were using aircraft to cross the vast North American continent.

The Boeing Company had not neglected the military and continued to supply fighter and trainer aircraft to the USAAC and US Navy. It also designed a sleek all-metal monoplane with retractable

Above: The Boeing 247 is being run up at RAF Mildenhall at the start of the MacRobertson Race to Australia. Parked alongside is the KLM DC-2, which came second.

Right: The flight deck of the Boeing 247.

Airlines were keen to put the Boeing 247 airliner into service. It is seen here in production.

The prototype Boeing 307 Stratoliner set the pattern followed by airliners to the present day.

undercarriage for the mail service. Called the Monomail, it first flew in May 1930 and, as the Model 221, went into service soon afterwards. Using the experience gained with the Model 221, Boeing designed and built a larger version for demonstration to the USAAC, which was suitably impressed and ordered an example for evaluation. It also ordered the monoplane P-26 Peashooter fighter into production for the Corps.

The flight deck of a Boeing 307 Stratoliner.

Modern Airliner

Having the military contracts enabled Boeing to expand its commercial operations further; other companies were added to the portfolio, and Boeing Air Transport and its associated airlines became United Air Lines. To serve in the enlarged airline, a new aircraft, the Boeing 247, was designed and built and a total of 60 examples were delivered to United within a year. The Boeing 247 made a complete break with the past, representing a new type of transport aircraft with which the earlier types were unable to compete. This advanced twin-engined airliner could cruise at 155mph, had a range of 485 miles and a service ceiling of 18,000ft.

United Air Lines had ordered the type off the drawing board, and the first 247 entered service in March 1933 and was put on the US transcontinental route, where it cut the journey time down to just under 20hrs, compared with the previous time of 27hrs. The shortcomings of the 247 were few and limited to operations from high and hot airports, where the fixed-pitch propellers impaired performance. Boeing introduced a new version, the 247D, which had variable-pitch Hamilton airscrews, increased fuel capacity, more power at higher altitudes, and various other improvements that increased the cruising speed to 189mph and the range to 745 miles. Most of the original 60 247s were modified to 247D standard, and an additional 15 were manufactured for other airlines, including Deutsche Luft Hansa. Passengers were offered even more comfort than previous Boeing airliners, and the 247 became the first airliner to fly a regular passenger transcontinental service in less than 20hrs. Certainly, the Boeing 247 can take its place as one of the great aircraft and may be seen as the true ancestor of all modern monoplane airliners.

A Transcontinental and Western Air (TWA, later Trans World Airlines) Stratoliner about to land. TWA bought five of the ten aircraft produced.

Transcontinental and Western Air (TWA, later Trans World Airlines) was anxious to obtain the Boeing 247, but the manufacturer did not have the capacity to build the quantity needed by TWA, as well as those required by United. Consequently, TWA issued its own specification for a three-engined airliner; it was still thought that three engines were safer than two, and various manufacturers came up with designs. It was, however, Donald Douglas who talked TWA's Charles Lindberg into buying the twin-engined Douglas DC-1, which offered better performance over the Boeing 247.

The Boeing 247 and the Douglas DC-1 and DC-2 were far more advanced than their contemporaries in Britain and Europe. Comparing the types operated by Imperial Airways over similar distances with those in service in the US is interesting, to say the least. The faster, quieter monoplanes, such as the de Havilland DH.91 Albatross and Armstrong Whitworth Ensign, did not arrive on the British scene until well into the 1930s, and the large Short flying boats, which have come to epitomize the so-called "golden days of air travel," were only in service for a brief period before the World War Two ceased operations.

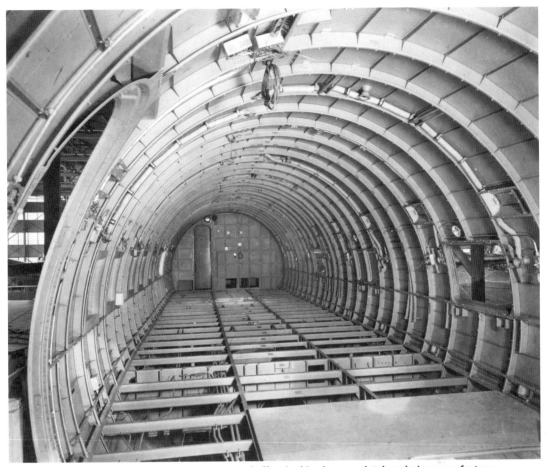

The spacious interior of a Stratoliner is seen to good effect in this photograph taken during manufacture.

Large Clipper

William Boeing retired from the company he had created in 1934 and dedicated himself to other business and leisure activities. His aircraft and airline companies carried on, and, in 1938, they fielded two exceptional models that would influence all future air travel. Flying boats had been designed, built and operated by various countries to open up air travel – water being more plentiful than purpose-built runways. Boeing had been working on a large flying boat and this came to fruition on June 7, 1938, when the Model 314 Clipper made its first flight.

Designed by Wellwood Beall, it beat the Sikorski and Martin designs for the lucrative Pan American (Pan Am) contract. Boeing produced a large four-engined aircraft that had a range of over 5,000 miles. When it first flew, it was the largest airliner in the world and went into Pan Am service in January 1939. *Yankee Clipper*, as the first aircraft was named, carried a crew of ten and had very comfortable seats in nine compartments on two decks for up to 74 passengers. For night flights, there were 36 berths, or 38 if convertible seats were installed in the central lounge area. Regular service on the New York to Marseilles via Lisbon route commenced in June 1939. A month later, routine flights to Southampton were inaugurated.

Boeing's other 1938 debutante was the Model 307 Stratoliner; it offered the same comfort levels as the 247 but was larger and powered by four engines. The Stratoliner was also the first US airliner to carry passengers in a pressurized cabin; this meant that the aircraft could fly at 20,000ft, above most turbulent weather conditions. First flown on December 31, 1938, the Model 307 could carry 33 passengers and had a range of over 2,000 miles. Unfortunately, World War Two put a stop to sales of the model and only ten were manufactured before Boeing turned its attentions to urgent military production of aircraft for the RAF and the USAAC.

The first of six Model 314 Clipper flying boats, NX18601, is seen during construction at Seattle.

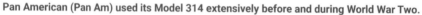

Pan American (Pan Am) used its Model 314 extensively before and during World War Two.

Chapter 2
Boeing in Wartime

Between the two wars, Boeing had not neglected its military aircraft business, and although contracts had slowed following the Armistice, there was still a requirement for the much smaller USAAC. Alongside this, the company carried on developing its commercial transport aircraft section.

Like many other countries that had come through World War One and the Depression, the United States was not alone in neglecting its armed forces. Europe had started rearming in the early 1930s,

US Army Air Forces (USAAF) Boeing B-17Fs were based in Britain for daylight raids on Germany. (USAF)

but America was slow, and lagged behind in terms of modern fast fighter, or pursuit, aircraft and its bomber force was small and antiquated. The situation lumbered on with no decisions being made for the future of the armed forces. This apathy was derived mainly by the fact that America was taking an increasingly isolationist stand and believed that, in being so far away from anyone else, it was safe from a direct attack by a hostile power. Coupled with this erroneous belief was a lack of interest being shown by many navy and army leaders and some government officials that there was no need for a modern defense capability. Aircraft were not regarded as a priority, and funds for developing a strong air force were not available in any quantity to make a difference.

A wake-up call came with the election of Franklin Delano Roosevelt as president in 1933; he brought a "New Deal" to bolster American industry and with it new equipment for the armed forces. The United States was woefully inadequate for any conflict that threatened its shores, and the new president was quick to address the situation. Although not all his chiefs-of-staff agreed with him, but with emerging problems on a global scale, they set about modernizing the military. At the time, America regarded any problems from Germany and Italy as something for Europe and Great Britain to deal with and did not want to be involved, but appropriate government departments monitored the situation as a matter of course. There was, however, concern for the growing military stance from Japan. Under a new government, the Japanese had started to modernize its enlarged army, navy and air force; new ships, military vehicles and aircraft were commissioned and a dialogue with Nazi Germany was started. Japan was showing signs of aggression and commentators were genuinely concerned about the situation in the Far East. America, as a whole, remained unconvinced, but some of its leaders were of the opinion that there could be trouble in the future, not necessarily directly between the United States and Japan, but problems that would need a strong US military.

Mass-produced by Boeing and other manufacturers, there were more than 13,000 B-17s built.

Boeing Responds

New specifications were issued by the US Army for land and aerial vehicles – the Air Corps (and later Air Force) was still part of the Army – and for new ships for the Navy. Boeing responded with designs for a new fighter and for a bomber. In May 1934, Boeing and Martin Aircraft were approached by the USAAC to build what were to be the first four-engine aircraft yet ordered by the Air Corps. Boeing showed its designs for such a type as the XB-15, and this was chosen for development. Meanwhile, Boeing had been at work with the Model 300 Stratoliner, and, alongside that model, it was developing a bomber variant as a private venture with the designation Model 299.

The large XB-15 was bypassed by the Model 299, which was drawn up to a 1933 USAAC requirement and funded by the company. Boeing was not in a strong financial position at the time and was gambling on its Model 299 four-engined bomber being accepted and ordered into production; if it failed, the company would face a bleak future. Boeing draftsmen, engineers, and builders worked all-hours to get the proposal ready. Their hard work paid off, they met the deadline of mid-1935 that had been set by the US Army, and the Type 299 made its first flight on July 28, 1935. It was successful and impressed the USAAC, which ordered evaluation examples and then placed a quantity order for what became the Boeing B-17 Flying Fortress. The sole XB-15 was converted for use as a cargo aircraft and used on long overseas routes in the South Pacific and elsewhere.

Boeing developed the Flying Fortress throughout the war and used build techniques that had also been applied to the Stratoliner, which would also play its part in the war effort. Turning the Boeing plants to the manufacture of B-17s for export and for the US Army occupied the factories throughout the war. The aircraft was ordered in quantity and to meet the demand, it had to be licensed to other

This restored Boeing 247 was painted in the United Air Lines livery.

aircraft manufacturers to meet the build quotas. By the time production ceased at the end of the war, nearly 13,000 B-17s of all models had been manufactured.

When the US entered the war in 1941, Boeing's two prewar land airliners, the Model 247 and Model 300 Stratoliner, were pressed into military service. Twenty-seven examples of the Model 247 were taken over and given the designation C-73 as troop transport aircraft, but they were found unsuitable for this purpose and were used in the training role and to ferry aircrew. The five Stratoliners that had been delivered to TWA were taken over and given the USAAC designation C-75. They were operated by TWA under contract to the USAAC Air Transport Command as VIP transports for the highest ranking civilian and military personnel. By VE-Day in May 1945, the five C-75s had, between them, made some 3,000 transatlantic crossings, logged 45,000 flight hours and flown about 7.5 million miles without mishap.

The Stratoliner was a useful aircraft in the role it played, as it could fly high above most of the weather encountered over the North Atlantic and out of reach of any enemy aircraft. Released from service, the aircraft were returned to Boeing to be rebuilt and returned to standard airline configuration for use by commercial operators following the cessation of hostilities. Data from the Model 300's transatlantic flights would prove useful for the next generation of Boeing airliners.

The Stratoliner was used by the US military as a transport and made several Atlantic crossings without incident.

By the last year of World War Two, USAAF aircraft were in bare metal finish, as seen on this aircraft.

Pan Am's first Boeing 314 is seen undergoing maintenance; the figures provide scale to this large flying boat.

Photographed on Southampton Water just before the war are two Imperial Airways C-Class flying boats and a Pan Am B314 Clipper.

Pushing the Boundaries

On January 29, 1940, a Request for Proposals was sent to five US aircraft manufacturers by the USAAC. The top-secret specification called for a bomber that had an unladen range of over 5,000 miles and one that could carry a full bomb and fuel load over a range of 2,000 miles from its operating base. In due course, design studies were submitted by Boeing, Consolidated, Douglas, and Lockheed; the last two subsequently withdrew from the competition.

As early as 1938, Boeing had proposed an improved version of the B-17 with a pressurized cabin, to make high altitude operations less demanding on the crew. At the time, there was no requirement for such an aircraft and the proposal remained on paper. However, the US Army encouraged Boeing to keep the design updated to keep up with the changing times that could warrant such an aircraft in the future. This head-start gave Boeing an advantage over the other contenders for the proposed long-range bomber.

The Seattle manufacturer quickly put in to place a design team under Edward Wells – who had led the B-17 design team – and submitted the Boeing Model 345 as a proposal for the long-range bomber. By now, the USAAC had been renamed the US Army Air Force (USAAF) and, on September 6, contracts were awarded to Boeing and Consolidated (now Convair) for the construction and development of two (later three) prototypes for evaluation.

Boeing was able to apply the experience gained with the pressurized Stratoliner to the new design. A three-section system was installed, with the pilots' flight deck and the waist gunner's position being

Pressurization enabled the B-29 to operate at an altitude of nearly 32,000ft.

pressurized and connected by a pressurized tunnel. The tail gunner's area was pressurized separately. Pressurization enabled the B-29 to operate at much higher altitudes than unpressurized bombers, such as the B-17 and B-24, then in service.

On September 21, 1942, the first prototype XB-29 was flown by Boeing test pilot Edmund "Eddie" Allen. Boeing was entering unchartered territory with the new bomber; it pioneered remote weapons stations that were computer operated; a new high efficiency wing (Model 117) was designed and fitted. The four Wright R3350-13 Double Cyclone engines had to be designed for operation at high altitude and were fitted with two General Electric turbochargers. The work on the B-29 was slowed down with the need to concentrate on building aircraft already in service, but after trials the aircraft was ordered into quantity production and 14 YB-29s were manufactured as service test aircraft. They were delivered to 58th Very Heavy Bombardment Wing towards the end of July 1943 for crew training. The unit had been formed on June 1, in advance of the first flight of the YB-29 on June 26.

The Boeing B-29 was the largest landplane built in the United States during World War Two and its most famous operation has to be the dropping of the atomic bombs on Japan in August 1945, which finally ended the war in the Far East. Boeing had benefited financially from the military contracts, and, in 1941, alongside the B-29, studies commenced of transport derivatives of the large bomber.

The Boeing B-29 was the first pressurized US bomber to go into service during World War Two.

Chapter 3

Enter the Stratocruiser

During the early years of World War Two, Boeing's several aircraft plants, as well as various subcontractors, were fully committed and working to capacity to meet the demands for B-17 Flying Fortresses and, from 1943, for the B-29 Superfortress. The design and engineering teams were confident with their products and could see future development of the B-29 and were encouraged by Boeing president Philip Johnson to consider the type as a troop transport.

Design work commenced using as many components from the B-29 as possible. Called Model 367, the aircraft retained the excellent B-29 Model 117 wing design, undercarriage and tail unit, but married onto the lower fuselage of the B-29 (suitably adapted) was a totally new pressurized and much larger upper fuselage. The engineers, including aerodynamicist Jack Steiner, who had worked on the B-29, developed a fuselage that was a pair of pressurized cylinders, which gave the Model 367 its distinctive "figure-eight" or "double-bubble" cross section. The lower of the two cylinders had roughly the same dimensions as the B-29's fuselage and was designed to be used as a cargo hold. Overlapping it by several feet, the larger upper cylinder was designed to accommodate up to 134 soldiers and their equipment or, as an airliner, 40–55 passengers in large comfortable first-class seats.

Brochures of the proposed troop transport were shown to the USAAF in January 1942, and it was sufficiently impressed to order three XC-97 prototypes. Work on the existing aircraft in-build remained a priority but Boeing allocated funds and personnel to develop the Model 367 XC-97.

Early bare metal finish Pan Am Stratocruiser N1041V *Strato Clipper* is readied for flight at London Airport.

American Overseas Airways bought the Stratocruiser for use on their domestic, as well as Atlantic, routes.

Design Differences

At the time, the design of Model 367 looked futuristic, and the data from wind tunnels showed that the aircraft would have a cruising speed that matched that of the B-29. Boeing concentrated its efforts on the military transport but allocated a few engineers to work on the differences needed for civil applications after the war. This was given the designation Type 377, and the engineering team, under Edward Wells and Wellwood Beall, was able to use data obtained from the military XC-97, which had flown on November 9, 1944. The two airframes were generally the same, with the different model numbers used mainly to distinguish the military from the civilian end user. The differences were primarily in avionics, interior layout, and the addition of clamshell doors and/or refueling gear on the Model 367.

The prototype XC-97 was powered by four 2,200hp Wright R-3350 engines, the same as used on the B-29. This aircraft and the other pre-production examples were fitted with a shorter fin and rudder from the B-29, but later production examples would be built with the enlarged fin and rudder from the B-50. The C-97 had clamshell doors under its tail, so a retractable ramp could be used to drive in cargo. An electrically operated cargo hoist ran along the entire length of the fuselage and also raised and lowered the ramp. On January 9, 1945, the first prototype, piloted by Major Curtin Reinhardt, flew from Seattle to Washington, DC, in 6hrs 4mins at an average speed of 383mph with 20,000lb of cargo, which was an impressive load at the time.

With the end of the war, there was no immediate need for the Model 367 and work slowed on the program. However, the aircraft was still required, and, late in 1945, the United States Air Force (USAF) ordered six YC-97s, three YC-97As and a YC-97B, all of which were delivered in a cargo/troop carrier configuration. These examples were used for evaluation purposes and one of the YC-97As (45-9595) was used on the Berlin Air Lift during April 1949, operating with 1st Strategic Support Squadron.

Boeing was given an order for 50 C-97As and 14 C-97Cs in 1948 and 1950, respectively. The recently formed Strategic Air Command (SAC) took over the single YC-97B as a flying command post with the designation VC-97D. Meanwhile, work on the commercial variant had not been forgotten.

Stratocruiser

Using the flight data from the XC-97, the Model 377 took shape at the Seattle facility and work on the Stratocruiser – a name chosen to denote the fact that it could fly high above weather and turbulence – was intensified. Wellwood Beall took a personal interest in making the interior cabin as comfortable as possible; he also took it upon himself to champion the new airliner. Brochures were dispatched to chief executives of US airlines to herald the new Stratocruiser and flights were arranged as required.

Pan American World Airways, under Juan Trippe, who had long championed Boeing aircraft, placed a first order for 20 Stratocruisers in 1945; a contract valued at US$24m. Other airlines also queued up to place orders for the Model 377: Scandinavian Airlines System (SAS) ordered four in February 1946 (these were not delivered and were taken over by British Overseas Airways Corporation [BOAC]);

This United Airlines Stratocruiser shows off to advantage the slim Boeing Model 117 wing that had been used on the B-29.

in March, Northwest Airlines became the first domestic American carrier to order the Stratocruiser. American Overseas Airlines and United also purchased the aircraft, as did BOAC; in August 1946, it placed an order for six aircraft to be used on the North Atlantic service. The Northwest and United Stratocruisers were built to a slightly different standard, the most obvious being that Northwest aircraft were fitted with all rectangular windows and an aft galley, and United aircraft had rectangular windows for the main cabin and round windows on the lower deck.

Though the Model 377 had been developed via the B-29 and Model 367, it had its share of teething troubles. The main problems arose from the more powerful and complicated 3,500hp Pratt & Whitney R-4360B Wasp Major radial engines with their General-Electric turbochargers and the hollow-steel, square-tipped Hamilton Standard propellers. On test, one propeller failure had ripped an engine off its mount and went spinning over the top of the aircraft. There were 28 cylinders per engine and two spark plugs for each cylinder; this totaled 224 plus for each aircraft, and it was discovered that if the engines were kept idling too long before take-off, the plugs gummed up with oil. When this happened, there was no alternative but to taxi back to the stand and have all the spark plugs changed. In the early days of test flights and ground running trials, the Boeing engineering team was very unhappy with the Stratocruiser's engines. They worked hard with Pratt & Whitney to overcome the problems that were largely, but not totally, sorted out. The plugs still oiled-up but not so badly; yet the maintenance

An early Pan Am Stratocruiser over Tower Bridge in London. Since this image was captured, the scene is much different.

Left: Looking aft at a Stratocruiser being built, the galley was at the rear of the cabin.

Below: Pan Am operated its Stratocruisers in base metal finish with titles for many years.

Transocean Air Lines was one of the many operators that bought second examples of the Stratocruiser for use on passenger and freight services.

hours and costs per engine remained high. This was one reason why so many of the major airlines did not buy the Stratocruiser. However, those that did were happy with the product and operated them successfully for many years.

Pan Am emerged after World War Two in a much stronger position than it had held in 1941; it had kept flying to various destinations throughout the war and, in due course, took over many routes from smaller airlines that had operational difficulties. Juan Trippe and William "Bill" Allen of Boeing got on well, and both men were totally dedicated to aviation. Trippe was interested in whatever aircraft Bill Allen had on offer and would send his team of engineers and test crew to fly the type and make their own notes, to the benefit of both companies. With the Stratocruiser, Trippe dispatched André Priester to Seattle to liaise with Jack Steiner and his team to get the aircraft just right for Pan Am; for example, the airline team found the ailerons were imprecise, and when the problems were investigated, Steiner's team agreed, and the problem was solved by Boeing aerodynamicist Joe Sutter.

Into Service

The first of a total of 56 Model 377s made its maiden flight on July 8, 1947, in Boeing markings and carrying the US civil registration NX90700. In 1950, after being used by Boeing as a flight test aircraft, it was reregistered N1022V and delivered to Pan Am as *Clipper Nightingale*. The first four Stratocruisers were also used for flight testing, and it was not until the fifth aircraft that Pan Am got its first Model 377.

Delivered to the airline as *Clipper America*, the Stratocruiser commenced revenue-earning flights on April 1, 1949, between Los Angeles and Honolulu, the airline's busiest route. Aircraft were supplied to be configured with 55–100 seats or 28 sleeper berths on the upper deck. There were 14 seats on the lower lounge deck. The standard accommodation for the Stratocruiser was 67 seats on the upper deck and the 14 lounge seats as previously noted. Pan Am Stratocruisers were fitted with seats on tracks so that they could be spaced according to the mix of first and tourist class passengers. This idea had been pioneered by the airline and was soon adopted universally. Ray Ireland, president of United Airlines, placed his order for the Stratocruiser when he saw its popularity in Pan Am service.

Airlines made a great deal of the aircraft's twin-deck and in their publicity material there was always a cutaway drawing showing the lower deck with passengers enjoying a drink while looking out of the windows at clouds far below.

All but nine of the 56 Stratocruisers were delivered to the airlines during 1949, and four of the remaining nine would be delivered in January 1950. The first non-Pan Am Model 377s were delivered to American Overseas Airlines and Northwest Airlines in June 1949. The last Model 377 was delivered in March 1950, by which time, it was estimated that the fleet had already carried 160,000 passengers more than nine million miles.

Airlines in the United States and abroad were now operating probably the most luxurious and comfortable airliner of the day. BOAC introduced its "Monarch" service to New York from London Heathrow on March 1, 1951; initially on a thrice-weekly basis but upgraded to a daily service from May 1. BOAC passengers paid a small additional charge for the privilege of travelling in the sumptuous cabin, while enjoying the standard of service that would be found in the best hotels and on board the luxury ocean liners that were still the preferred mode of transatlantic travel.

A menu card from a BOAC Stratocruiser of 1951 informs us that, following cocktails, dinner consisted of caviar, turtle soup, cold Inverness salmon, and spring chicken with Wiltshire bacon and peas. A selection of vegetables was also served. Dessert consisted of Hampshire strawberries with fresh double cream, followed by biscuits, cheese, and fresh fruit. Fine wines and champagne were complimentary and served throughout dinner, and liqueurs were served after dinner either at the passengers' seats or in the lower deck cocktail lounge that was accessed via a spiral staircase. The lower deck could also be used as a lounge or for 14 seats or as a bar and rest room. It was novel and attractive to airline operators and passengers alike; it was also something that the rival Douglas and Lockheed airliners lacked.

Sleeper berths were available on the Monarch service, and they were prepared by the stewardesses who made the beds up with blankets, pillows, and fresh linen sheets. A small surcharge was made for the sleeper service. BOAC gave men a special Monarch silk tie and ladies received various toiletries, such as perfume and soap, etc. Pan Am noted the success of BOAC's Monarch service and introduced its own version soon afterwards.

Known as the "President" and "President Special" services, the US airline made a charge of US$50 each way and passengers were provided with a seven course meal, champagne, and a sleeper berth that was equally as good as that of BOAC. Ladies were presented with orchids and perfume and gentlemen were given a complimentary cigar. There were five cabin staff to attend to 47 passengers, and it was even possible to hire a two- or four-berth stateroom in the forward portion of the cabin. Pan Am also made good use of the lower deck in a similar manner to BOAC with a cocktail lounge or additional seats where passengers could relax. It is worth noting that the fare from London to New York and return in 1950 was $630 during the peak season and $466 off peak. There were magazine articles in the popular press on both sides of the Atlantic about the Stratocruiser and its remarkable twin-deck passenger arrangements. We take this sort of travel for granted today, but 70 years ago, it was a novelty and out of the reach of the average person.

The Stratocruiser was in the news when, at midnight on October 8, 1951, their Royal Highnesses Princess Elizabeth and the Duke of Edinburgh boarded the BOAC Stratocruiser flagship *Canopus* for a flight to Montréal via Gander, Newfoundland, on the first leg of a state visit to Canada. It was the first Royal Tour to depart from Heathrow and also the first occasion that members of the British Royal Family had crossed the Atlantic by air. The resulting news coverage of the flight brought the aircraft to a wider audience and boosted BOAC's profile.

Robert Lamson, Boeing test pilot on the Stratocruiser program, joined several crews on the type to see how they were adapting to flying the airliner on scheduled services. His report to head office is one of praise from the pilots and engineers; they liked the Stratocruiser and were getting seven hours' utilization a day, which included time spent in the maintenance hangar. The aircraft was singled out for its ease of flying; some of the pilots making these reports had been flying since the 1920s on a variety of different types, so they knew what to expect. Lamson also noted the fact that American Overseas Airlines instructed its pilots to fly the airliner across the Atlantic manually (not on autopilot), and that even after a three-hour stint at the controls, the pilot was not fatigued.

Pan Am and BOAC continued operations across the Atlantic, and during 1950, additional fuel tanks were fitted in the wings to make the journey nonstop. Services were popular, but cheaper flights from TWA, El Al Israeli Airlines, and others meant that the Stratocruisers had to be reconfigured to carry more passengers, and the sleeper berths were not always available on every service. BOAC did operate the Stratocruiser on other routes to Africa and the Middle East, but as the Bristol Britannia and de Havilland Comet 4 came into service, the slower piston-engined type was nearing the end of its

The first Stratocruiser carrying Boeing in-house livery shows off its lines in this superb photograph.

Two views of a Northwest Airlines Stratocruiser – note the square passenger windows that were fitted to this variant.

days. BOAC Stratocruiser operations came to an end on May 31, 1959, when G-ANTY flew from Accra via Kano and Barcelona to London.

The Stratocruiser's career as a passenger carrier with its original first tier operators ended on September 15, 1960, when the last Northwest Stratocruiser touched down at Minneapolis-St Paul after a flight from New York. It was not, however, the end of the type, as they were quickly acquired by smaller airlines. The luxury trimmings were deleted, and seats for up to 112 passengers were fitted in their place. Línea Internacional Aérea of Ecuador was among the many airlines that operated the aircraft, and Rutas Aéreas Nacionales SA of Venezuela and Transocean also purchased secondhand examples of the Stratocruiser and used them successfully for many years on cargo operations. The Stratocruiser may only have had a short commercial life, but it is remembered with affection by those passengers who were cosseted by the airlines and who dreamed in a comfortable bed as the miles drifted by.

Those who maintained the type found it troublesome and time-consuming, but old engineers from BOAC still have a fond spot for the Stratocruiser. Pilots liked it, and, as many of them had flown heavy bombers during the war, they found the aircraft easier to fly and lighter on the controls. A former BOAC captain remarked that: "After the Argonaut anything would have been better! The Strat was good and easy to fly, it was responsive and had more than enough power to shift the load. It was comfortable for the crew, and we had more space on the flight deck than on other types. In fact, the 707 was cramped in comparison."

A British Overseas Aircraft Corporation (BOAC) Stratocruiser undergoes routine maintenance at the airline's hangar at London Airport.

Above: The prototype Boeing Stratocruiser being prepared for another test flight from Boeing Field, Seattle.

Left: A Hamilton Standard propeller is refitted to the engine of a BOAC Stratocruiser at London Airport.

Opposite above: Stratocruisers under construction at the Boeing plant at Renton in Washington State.

Opposite below: A long queue of people gathers to see on board this American Overseas Airways Boeing Stratocruiser.

The bare metal finish of Pan Am was replaced with a new white and blue livery.

In Military Service

Deliveries of production C-97 Stratofreighters commenced in 1950 and with a useful payload of 35,000lb, they were the first of the heavy-lift cargo aircraft in the USAF. The C-97 transports were assigned primarily to the Military Air Transport Service (MATS) and could carry two standard US trucks, towed artillery or light tracked vehicles. The pressurized cabin was something that had not been encountered by the military before and made long-range missions more comfortable for the crew and passengers. By 1950, the type was in action during the Korean War; apart from supply deliveries, it was used to evacuate casualties. Sometimes the C-97s flew at tree-top height to evade the enemy ground fire. The capacious cargo hold could house 96 infantry or 69 patients with medical staff; critically wounded soldiers were flown from staging areas in Japan to hospitals in Hawaii or the mainland United States. With a top speed of 375mph and cruise at 300mph up to a ceiling of 35,000 feet and range of 4,300 miles, the C-97 was a valuable asset to the US forces in Korea. Some C-97s were configured to carry 134 fully equipped soldiers or 83 stretcher cases with four attendants.

During the early stages of the Korean War, the Stratofreighter was fitted with AN/APS42 six-unit radar assembly housed in a radome under the nose of the aircraft. This addition made the C-97 the first US production transport to carry radar as standard equipment. Primarily a navigation aid, the radar gave a picture of the terrain over which the aircraft was passing and provided navigational checkpoints, such as mountains, lakes, and cities. It also gave the aircraft the ability to fly in all weathers and with the radar in operation, gave the pilot a warning of other aircraft – friendly or otherwise – in the area. Over the ensuing years, the radar was upgraded and lodged in the distinctive nose housing.

With growing concern about the Cold War, the USAF expanded long-range bomber operations within SAC and sought to extend the operating range of its aircraft. In-fight refueling had been pioneered by Alan Cobham in Britain between the wars, and by 1950, was a viable system. The USAF used the basics of Cobham's Flight Refuelling Company's system and developed a version of its own.

As a dedicated air tanker, the C-97 was chosen by the USAF, and, in 1951, 60 in-flight refueling aircraft were ordered under the designation KC-97E, and another 159 as KC-97F. All of these aircraft were, in theory, capable of being converted to the transport role, but with the rear cargo doors sealed.

Boeing received a further order for 592 KC-97Gs for delivery between 1951 and 1953; these were dedicated dual-role tanker/transports. They had accommodation for troops or stretchers on the top deck without having to remove the refueling tanks located on the lower deck. In the dual role of tanker/transport, the KC-97G was capable of taking off with a 175,000lb overall weight. However, in order that the KC-97G could keep pace with the faster jets like the B-47 Stratojet bomber, 82 were fitted with a pair of Pratt & Whitney J47-GE-25A turbojets to supplement the power of their piston engines. The turbojets were located under the wings in pods on either side, and the type was designated KC-97L. Another example of the KC-97G was fitted with four 5,700shp Pratt & Whitney YT34 turboprops in place of the piston engines; it made its first flight on April 19, 1955. Other examples were also converted with the more powerful, fuel-efficient and reliable turboprop engines. Boeing did show plans for a Stratofreighter with swept wings and four Pratt & Whitney XJ-57-P turbojet engines housed in twin pods under the wings, but this remained a concept and was not proceeded with, but the idea was not forgotten, as we shall see.

The military C-97 troop transport had basic seats in the center, as well as along each side for service personnel.

The distinctive "double bubble" cross section of the Stratocruiser/C-97 fuselage can be seen clearly in this production image.

This front view of a military C-97 shows the slim wings and unusual fuselage to advantage.

More Power

As the Boeing KC-135 Stratotanker jet refueling aircraft entered USAF service in the late 1950s, the KC-97s were gradually withdrawn to other USAF commands and the Air National Guard, with which they served until the 1980s. However, the KC-97 gained a new lease of life when the KC-135s were concentrated in Southeast Asia during the Vietnam War. The KC-97s took over duties with the USAF in Europe and elsewhere in the world as the KC-135s were moved to the Vietnam theater.

Other variants of the C-97 that were developed included air-sea rescue and Electronic Intelligence (ELINT) gathering examples. Unlike the Stratocruiser, the Stratofreighter went into quantity production, and within ten years of the first prototype's flight, Boeing had produced the 500th example, a KC-97K, on February 8, 1954, at its Renton plant. A Boeing publication from the time states:

> In the course of its ten-year span since the first experimental XC-97 of 1944, the Stratofreighter has done a lot of growing, in every aeronautical sense of the word. Tankers now rolling off the Renton production line can take-off with a 175,000-pound over-all weight. The original "97" had a gross limit of 120,000-pounds. More than 300 major improvements have been incorporated into the Stratofreighter during those ten years. Changes include a stronger, lighter wing; a strengthened fuselage and landing gear; an increase in engine take-off power from 8,000 hp to 14,000 hp; and most important of all, the development of the transport airplane into a tanker.

At the time that "Miss 500," as the workers at Renton affectionately called the aircraft, rolled off the line, Boeing was producing one C-97 per working day to meet the government contracts. As the orders were filled, production slowed down in favor of extending delivery of the same number of KC-97s over

A C-97 tanker lowers a refueling boom to a B-50 Superfortress bomber. The family resemblance between the two aircraft is clearly visible.

The interior of a C-97 in the CASEVAC role with stretchers and medical personnel in attendance.

Three great Boeings together at Renton: the C-97/ Stratocruiser, Dash Eighty and B-52 Stratofortress prototype.

a longer period of time. The final, 888th example of the C-97 series rolled out of the Renton factory on July 18, 1956 – the same day as the first jet-powered KC-135 emerged at the same facility.

The aircraft was mainly employed by the USAF, but Israel also made use of the type when it was unable to acquire the C-130 Hercules. Buying civilian Stratocruisers, Israeli Aircraft Industries adapted them as transports by using C-97 tail sections with the loading ramp and clamshell doors. They were known as "Anak," which is Hebrew for "giant." Three Stratocruisers were fitted with a swing-tail, and two others were modified to carry underwing hose-reel refueling pods. They were later joined by two KC-97Gs with the flying boom aerial refueling system. Precisely what electronic equipment was installed on the Israeli Stratocruiser/C-97s is unknown, but they were used in the ELINT role to gather intelligence, reconnaissance, and ECM missions; one was shot down near the Suez Canal by an Egyptian SA-2 Guideline missile on September 17, 1971.

End of the Line

Even though the Stratocruiser was no longer flying passengers, some aircraft did soldier on as cargo transports in South America and Mexico, and they were often seen in Miami alongside the many piston-engine airliners that also found a new lease of life. With the aircraft's useful cargo capacity, it was no surprise that another role beckoned.

Nine C-97s were bought by Aero Space Lines, which made a speciality of converting the type and rebuilding them as large cargo carriers, tripling their internal volume to 22,500 cubic feet. Powered

A C-97 of the Military Air Transport Service (MATS) is seen with four turboprops in place of the piston engines. The radar radome is visible on the lower section of the nose.

43

by four 4,912shp Allison 501-D22C turboprops in place of the radial piston engines and known as Guppies and Super Guppies, they were used to transport large and heavy structures around the world. BAE Systems/Airbus Industries used an example for many years to carry sections of Airbus airliners between the various factories for final assembly at Toulouse.

While its Stratocruiser had brought a new level of comfort to air travel, Boeing suffered from comparisons to rival airliners. Although not as plush as the Model 377, Douglas' DC-6/DC-7 and Lockheed's Constellation carved out the larger market share. Boeing reputedly lost US$7m on the Model 377 Stratocruiser (it would make some of this up with the military variant) and was regarded to be out of the commercial airliner business as a result.

However, Boeing was not about to leave the scene. Its deep involvement with the USAF B-47 Stratojet and B-52 Stratofortress programs would see the company on to its next commercial aviation project.

To assist the heavily loaded C-97 tankers, two small turbojets were mounted under each wing for extra power.

Chapter 4

Prototype and Design

Britain had seized the lead in jet airliner travel with the de Havilland Comet, which first flew in July 1949. This aircraft left all others in its wake and BOAC, in pioneering jet airline service, had a distinct advantage over all other airlines. A "catch-up" race began, with airlines clamoring to order the Comet and aircraft manufacturers trying to get their own pure-jet designs from paper to metal. However, a major blow struck the aircraft industry and the airlines when several BOAC Comets crashed. The Comet fleets were grounded, and a full-scale inquiry commenced at the Royal Aircraft Establishment at Farnborough in Hampshire, to determine the cause of the crashes.

Nothing was hidden, and the full text of the enquiry was produced for all to benefit. Across the Atlantic, Boeing had been following the case closely as it had a design for a jet airliner on the drawing board. Some manufacturers shied away from the jet concept and concentrated with their successful piston-engine-powered designs; Douglas and Lockheed in the US, especially, were late in embracing jet airliner technology, but in Britain, Bristol and de Havilland persisted with the jet-powered airliner.

Boeing's initial studies into jet airliners began as early as 1946, when the company evaluated turbojet- and turboprop-powered versions of the C-97 and Stratocruiser. When the war ended, Boeing's chief aerodynamicist, George Schairer – who had designed the highly-efficient Model 117 wing for the B-29 – traveled to Germany with the US Army Scientific Advisory Group to evaluate German scientific and technical data and, if possible, meet and talk to some of those who had been involved. Schairer

An early sketch for a Boeing jet airliner; it shows a Stratocruiser fuselage with a swept wing housing four turbojets in pairs.

The Boeing Dash Eighty under construction – as a possible military aircraft, two cargo doors were installed. No passenger windows were fitted to the prototype

visited the former Messerschmitt factory and saw for himself how effective the swept-back wing of the Me 262 fighter had been. His thoughts on wing design were changed immediately, and when he got back to Seattle, he was enthusiastic about the use of a swept-wing. Schairer convinced Ed Wells, who was in overall charge of the Model 367 development project, about the need to redesign the aircraft. Wells went to Bill Allen, who had become president of Boeing in 1945, and showed him the findings. Allen had the task of convincing the USAF that its new jet bomber, then on the drawing board, would be more efficient with a swept-wing.

Military minds are always wary of new ideas, and, at first, the USAF was no different, but after due consideration, it agreed to the change and Boeing got on with Model 448, drawings of which were shown in September 1945. Given the go-ahead, Wells and his team continued to refine the designs until they arrived at Model 450; the USAF ordered two prototypes and assigned the XB-47 designation to the aircraft. On December 17, 1947, the first XB-47 Stratojet made its maiden flight.

When Allen took charge of Boeing, he found that almost all of the government contracts had been canceled, as there was no longer any requirement for a large bomber fleet. Indeed, Allen had to lay off over 38,000 workers from the various Boeing plants in an effort to keep the company solvent. Gradually, new contracts were issued, first for the B-50, an improved version of the B-29, and later for the C-97. With the successful flight trials of the XB-47, the USAF issued production contracts for the B-47 Stratojet, which would ultimately be produced in far larger numbers than any other American bomber.

An artist's illustration from a company release shows a Boeing 707 in Braniff Airways livery.

Right: Boeing chief test pilot Alvin "Tex" Johnston was the first to fly the Dash Eighty. (Boeing)

Below: The Dash Eighty was rolled out May 15, 1954, in front of thousands of invited guests and press from around the world.

Working on the Airliner

At the time that Boeing were developing the jet-powered airliner concept, there was no interest from either military or civilian quarters on the various drawing board and wind tunnel models that were shown. Nevertheless, Boeing concluded that there was a requirement for such an aircraft and decided to continue with the concept as a private venture. Although the Stratocruiser had not sold and made a loss, the government C-97 and XB-47 contracts meant that Boeing was in a better financial position and could allocate funds and personnel to the airliner program.

Over 150 configurations were studied as the team, under Ed Wells, made their various calculations and designs; the Stratocruiser with standard straight wings carrying jet and/or turboprop engines gained a swept-wing, not unlike that of the XB-47 with four turbojets in pods under the wing. Given the designation Model 367-64 and 367-71, they featured 25 degrees of sweepback on the wings, and models were made for wind tunnel tests. The data was compared with the 35-degree sweep on the XB-47, and a new model was made of a modified 367 fuselage with a redesigned nose and with low-mounted wings emerged in late 1951. The wing of the new design was thicker than that of the 367-64 and featured a sweepback of 35 degrees, which was much more efficient and remarkable for a proposed commercial aircraft. This made the new aircraft closer aerodynamically with the B-47 Stratojet, which had flown in December 1947, than with the C-97. The bulbous Stratocruiser fuselage was also slimmed down and lost its "double-bubble" look.

However, Boeing did not want the fact that it was engaged with a jet airliner design to leak out, so it chose to designate the project as an extension of the Model 367 Stratofreighter program. Consequently, America's first jet airliner was the Boeing Model 367-80, known generally within the company as the "Dash Eighty." Further refining of the design continued, and on May 18, 1952, Bill Allen gave the go-ahead for the construction of a jet prototype to demonstrate the feasibility of a jet airliner to the skeptical US airlines; a jet tanker for SAC and a jet troop transport/freighter for MATS. The USAF still needed to be convinced, even though it had embraced jet technology for its bomber fleet.

In August 1952, the company announced publicly that it would be building a prototype of "an entirely new jet transport" but released no other details about the aircraft at the time. It also announced that it would be investing US$15m of its own funds. A section of the Renton plant was walled off to keep out prying eyes, and work on building the prototype commenced. Boeing already had experience with building jet aircraft from the successful B-47 Stratojet, which was in service with the USAF's SAC. It had also built and flown the YB-52 – later B-52 Stratofortress – prototype in April 1952, so the task ahead was not as daunting as it would have been for a workforce without the necessary experience. Douglas Aircraft, meanwhile, had also announced that it would be building a jet transport as the DC-8, but in the event did not start work on building a prototype until the airlines placed firm orders. It was still making and selling the successful piston-engined DC-7C at the time.

At first, Boeing had designed the mounting of the four engines to be in double pods, as used on the inboard pylons of the B-47, but the decision was soon taken to install the powerplants in single pods for safety and structural benefits. In a double pod, the failure of one engine may compromise the continued operation of the adjacent unit, and four pods provided better and even weight distribution along the wing, allowing a lighter structure. Interestingly, Boeing did not patent the design of having engines mounted on pylons under the wings, and this method has been followed by almost all aircraft manufacturers since that time. Chosen to power the Dash Eighty was the 11,000lb static thrust Pratt & Whitney JT3P twin-spool turbojets, the civilian version of the military J52 as fitted to the B-52. This was a shrewd move as the engines would have been thoroughly proven – at US government expense – before the JT3P was ready to be fitted to the Dash Eighty. Although the Comet had entered passenger service, there was still resistance in the US amongst airline operators and passengers about jet engine reliability. However, Boeing would be able to use the success of the B-47 and B-52 powerplants to advertise its jet airliner.

First metal was cut at Renton in October 1952 and the project team, led by Ed Wells and including Jack Steiner, George Schairer, and Maynard Pennell, set to work on the complex task ahead. The aircraft was being built in secrecy, and all that had been released was the fact that it was a jet-powered Stratocruiser that would be offered as a freighter, troop transport, and airliner. To address the first application, the prototype was constructed with full-size forward and aft freight loading doors and with a cargo floor installed; there were no windows or seats fitted for an airliner configuration.

At the time, Boeing stated that:

In presenting its jet transport, Boeing has chosen to begin by building a prototype because this method brings, for both customer and manufacturer, several advantages that can be obtained in no other way. For one thing, the prototype experience should enable Boeing to deliver its first operational production model at least eighteen months earlier than would be possible without that experience.

In building a prototype the experience on the basic design reduces tooling and manufacturing costs on subsequent airplanes. Specifically, the building of the prototype has provided first-hand knowledge of the problems, the solutions, the techniques of tooling for and manufacturing of any production models which may follow.

A Boeing worker attaching some of the hundreds of miles of wires and cables for installation in the Dash Eighty.

In 1991, the restored Dash Eighty made several appearances over Seattle to commemorate Boeing's 75th anniversary.

Inside the screened-off area at the Renton plant, the Dash Eighty, now painted, nears completion.

Outside the Renton plant, the prototype Boeing 707 is prepared for ground running trials before the first flight.

This photograph shows the full-size wooden mock-up of the Dash Eighty, which was built in great secrecy at Renton during 1952.

More than 21,000 hours was spent on wind tunnel tests of various models of multi-jet aircraft, and with data from some 5,000 hours of test flying of the B-47 and B-52 bombers, Boeing built up a wealth of experience that was applied to the Model 367-80. By March 1954, Boeing had produced over 600 examples of the B-47 Stratojet, and this further enhanced its experience of manufacturing large jet aircraft on a substantial scale.

First Flight

Work on the Dash Eighty was completed at Renton, and, on May 15, 1954, amid great fanfare, the prototype was rolled out from behind the enclosed area of the factory into the sunshine. Apart from senior Boeing executives and those working on the aircraft, this was the first time that anyone not involved with the project had seen the new jet transport. Thousands of Renton employees, invited guests, and the world's press were there; William Boeing made a rare visit to the company he had founded some 40 years earlier. Mrs. Bertha Boeing cracked a bottle of champagne on the nose of the cream and brown painted prototype and said: "I am not naming one aircraft today but three airplanes for tomorrow. The Stratotanker, Stratofreighter and Stratoliner."

The assembled guests were impressed by what they saw: the 136ft-long airliner with its dramatically swept back wings of 130ft was unlike anything else that had been seen before. Boeing had taken a massive gamble with the aircraft, there were no orders from the military or the commercial sector when it rolled the prototype out. All it could do was to get on with the first flight and work towards certification.

A superb image of the Dash Eighty at Renton on May 15, 1954, when the aircraft was shown to the public for the first time.

Following the roll-out, the aircraft, registered N70700, began a series of ground running tests for the engines, as well as high-speed taxi runs to check the control surfaces, braking, and other associated factors before the aircraft could attempt its first flight. This was delayed when, on May 21, during a braking test, the port main undercarriage attachment failed, and the aircraft's No. 1 engine nacelle and left wing tip struck the ground. Damage was not extensive, but testing had to stop while the repairs were carried out. The opportunity to strengthen the undercarriage was taken at the time.

For the maiden flight, Alvin "Tex" Johnston, Boeing chief test pilot, who had seen the B-47 and B-52 bombers through their test programs, was chosen to fly the Dash Eighty with Richards Loesch as copilot. On July 15, 1954, the two men climbed on board the aircraft at Renton and, following cockpit checks, started the engines. Johnston eased off the brakes and taxied towards the runway; at 1414hrs local, the Dash Eighty became airborne in less than 2,100ft of the 5,400ft runway at Renton. Although capable of taking off with 190,000lb, the prototype weighed in at 110,000lb, which included 3,400lb of flight test equipment. During the 2hr 24min-flight, Johnston carried out high- and low-speed handling tests and landed back at the airfield to a tremendous welcome. He commented to Allen: "The airplane's handling characteristics are very good. It wanted to climb like a rocket and we had to throttle back to keep within airspeed limits for this first flight. We reached 20,000ft in fifteen minutes, but we can do better!"

The prototype now commenced a series of flight trials, and Boeing hoped that orders would be forthcoming. General Curtis LeMay, Commander of SAC, flew on board N70700 and was sufficiently impressed enough to consider it for the tanker role, for which Lockheed's L-193 design had already been chosen, but that was still on the drawing board. The USAF ordered 29 KC-135 tankers on August 3, 1954, as an interim measure. Boeing referred to the new variant as the Model 717-100 and

In 1959, the prototype Boeing 707 was used as a test bed and was fitted with a nose radome to house the Bendix AN/AMQ-15 weather radar.

the USAF designated it KC-135A Stratotanker. Fortuitously, Boeing had kept abreast of the USAF tanker requirements and had designed a flight refueling boom that had been developed to simplify the rapid transfer of fuel from tanker to receiver. A non-operational example was later fitted to the prototype for flight trials.

Two days after the USAF order had been placed, following a short local flight, the prototype's brakes failed on touch-down; Johnston elected to cut the engines and steer the aircraft onto the grass to slow it down. Unfortunately, there were some concrete slabs hidden in the long grass; the nose gear made contact and collapsed. The damage was not extensive, but it kept the prototype grounded until September 20.

When testing resumed, Johnston wrote at length about the flights in the Boeing house journal:

> In our first 26 flights, we totaled 43 hours and 27 minutes. We proved that we have an airplane that should be leader in its field for a good many years to come. I can safely say that this airplane is not likely to be outperformed by anything this side of the supersonic era. The 707 can operate from any landing strip suitable for a large piston-engine transport. In fact, the 707 can operate more safely, as it can climb faster and clear obstacles more rapidly. The 707s ability to get to high altitude in a hurry is also important because greater fuel economies are made at high altitude. On occasion, getting upstairs rapidly for a refueling rendezvous will be a military asset, too.
>
> As a military tanker this airplane will be able to go out on missions with the B-52s. B-47s and jet fighters and refuel them under the conditions of speed and altitude best suited for these receivers. These points were initially demonstrated to our own satisfaction by a "formating" check flight with a Boeing B-52 Stratofortress. We made as many tests as we could on each flight.

Several airline executives flew on the Dash Eighty; here, a group waits to board via the large cargo door.

The Dash Eighty comes in to land after (probably) its maiden flight, when it was accompanied by a Beech 18 photographic aircraft.

It was on this basis that the airplane's loading and other factors were established for that flight. The program proceeded very smoothly because the 707's fine performance throughout helped to make our work easier.

Availability was not questioned; the 707 made 18 flights in nine days and was airborne for a total of 26hrs and 37mins. The aircraft and the engines remained serviceable, which for an experimental aircraft of that time, was quite exceptional.

Pan Am to the Rescue

Boeing had intended to keep the KC-135 variant as standard as possible so that as much tooling as possible could be used for the commercial airliner. This task was complicated by the USAF insisting that the Dash Eighty be able to take the standard US military pallet; this meant the aircraft, which was then the same width as the Stratocruiser at 132in, had to be increased by 8in. The four seats with an aisle gave way to five, three and two, abreast for an airliner. This increase in width was agreed, and the fuselage depth was also increased by 2in to 164in for the KC-135. Plans to produce the aircraft went ahead with these modifications, and Boeing started to tool up for an aircraft that had only been ordered in small numbers, though the USAF were likely to enlarge its requirements. To gain sales, the aircraft had to be ordered by the three leading US airlines: Pan Am, United and American. If they bought the 707, others would follow their lead. Everyone seemed reluctant, even though the airline executives had seen the prototype, some had flown on board, and they knew all about the jet. The snag was that Boeing was not known as an airliner manufacturer, that was Lockheed's and Douglas's territory, and Douglas was known to be building a larger jet airliner.

Then, on October 13, 1956, Juan Trippe from Pan Am, who had been a Boeing man since the interwar years, made the launch order for 20 B707s for delivery in October 1958. He also ordered 25 Douglas DC-8s at the same time, although this aircraft was still being built and was two years away from making its maiden flight. He wanted to be the first with a jet airliner and intended to operate the 707 until the DC-8 became available.

Details on the DC-8 were sketchy and little was known about it at the time, but then Maynard Pennell (a structures specialist who had joined Boeing from Douglas) saw a mock-up of a short section of cabin for the DC-8 made by United Airlines that led straight into a similar short section of a 707 cabin. Pennell had gone to United to sell them the Boeing airliner. Now he was faced with a far more spacious DC-8 interior and no order from United Airlines. United had been quite clear that it did not want the 707, and "Pat" Patterson, United's president, said he did not like the numbers "707" and United became launch customer for the DC-8. Later, when Patterson changed his mind and added the 707 to the fleet, it was called the 720 just for United.

Pernell was deeply concerned about United's attitude and by the mock-ups that he had seen. He took his findings to the Boeing board. Bill Allen listened and made the decision: the Douglas DC-8's 147in-wide cabin as depicted by United Airlines dictated that the 707 would have to be wider still; he added one inch to make the 707 cabin 148in wide. They could now seat six abreast in groups of three seats with a central aisle. Pan Am accepted the change, and brochures were sent out to other US airlines. Cyrus Smith, president of American Airlines, met Bill Allen on November 8, 1955, to discuss the 707 and at the end of the meeting, he signed an order for 30 aircraft. Finally, the gamble was paying off and orders were coming in, albeit slowly. Douglas was probably mistaken by not getting the DC-8 flying sooner, and though it made 556 examples of the airliner, it was half the number of commercial Boeing 707s that were sold.

To showcase the airliner, Boeing commissioned Frank del Giudice, from the famous US design house Walter Dowin Teague and Associates, to construct a full-size mockup of the 707 interior. Designs were made and color schemes chosen, and in great secrecy, a passenger cabin, complete with lavatories, rest areas, galleys, and seats was built at the cost of US$500,000, in a former coffee warehouse in Manhattan, New York. For three weeks, airline executives from around the world were wined and dined at the Waldorf Astoria Hotel in New York before being taken by limousine to the warehouse on Eleventh Avenue. They ascended to the eighth floor in a freight lift and on leaving were immediately in an airport departure lounge. Announcements were made that the "707 Superjet was ready for boarding" and the VIPs were escorted through a door and into the mock-up of the airliner cabin. The "passengers" fastened their safety belts and were treated to the sounds of four Pratt & Whitney JT3 engines starting up; the "Captain" announced that they would be cruising at 39,000ft at 590mph and stewardesses served the assembled guests cocktails. It was a gimmick and unlike anything Boeing had ever done in the past; it usually shied away from such theatricals, but needs must, and it had to sell the Boeing 707 to survive.

Frank del Giudice came up with a concept that was unlike the previous generation of airliners, and he, more or less, established the pattern that has been followed for airline interiors since. He also designed "snap-in" plastic panels that replaced the cloth covering that had been the usual until then. The panels could be printed especially for each airline with their logos and designs to make them different from each other. They were hard wearing and easier to keep clean; they were also lighter and saved weight. Overhead lockers and subdued lighting were further innovations from del Giudice. His choice of furnishings and colors were universally admired and certainly did much to sell the 707 to

The Dash Eighty was used for various trials and is seen here with a water spray rig installed in front of engine No. 3.

Full flaps as the Dash Eighty comes in to land after another test flight from Boeing Field, Seattle.

the airline executives who visited the mock-up. The use of modern materials meant that the interior of the airliner looked smart and required less maintenance than the current generation of piston-engine airliners. The seats were on tracks and could be removed quickly for cleaning and for reconfiguration as required depending on traffic density.

Testing the Prototype

Johnston continued to test the prototype and famously rolled it – a 1g maneuver that placed no stress on the airframe – but was told by Allen never to do it again. He did not want potential airliner buyers thinking that Boeing aircraft were tested by irresponsible pilots. Most of the test flights were of less than 2hrs in duration, and the aircraft stayed in North America, where various weather conditions could be found. In 1955, a total of 222 flights were made logging some 268 flight hours; the following year, it logged 284 hours and made 237 flights. Being a non-standard aircraft, the prototype was never fitted out as an airliner but was used for a variety of tasks during its long life with the company. The aircraft was used for various aspects of testing for Boeing, including trials with other engines, wing, tailplane, and flap configurations. When Boeing was experimenting with its proposed supersonic transport (SST) as a rival for Concorde, N70700 was fitted with a long instrument-filled nose probe. Data from these trials was useful in the company's work on large transport aircraft as well.

Notably, in 1959, the 707 prototype was fitted with a fixed 16-wheel main undercarriage and four-wheel nose gear, for trials for the very large aircraft program. This later became the C-5 Galaxy, and the trials, conducted at Harper Dry Lake in California, involved several take-offs and landings. Following the trials, the fixed gear was removed, the standard undercarriage attached, and the aircraft was flown back to Boeing at Seattle. That same year, N70700 was used to test the Bendix AN/AMQ-15 weather reconnaissance system that was housed in a large nose radome that contained the storm detection radar equipment.

In late 1960, N70700 was fitted with four Pratt & Whitney JT3D-1 turbofans for trials; two years later, the aircraft was fitted with a rear mounted Pratt & Whitney JT8D engine for tests for the Boeing 727. The jet efflux from the fifth engine was directed over the tailplane via a duct pipe. Boeing had so far mounted engines in pods under the wings, this was to change with the B727 when all three engines were mounted at the rear. Trials with N70700 gave Boeing engineers the required data for the engine location of the 727, which used a developed version of the 707 fuselage. Automatic Landing Systems (ALS) were installed in the Dash Eighty in 1969 for trials with the Federal Aviation Authority (FAA), and various fits for the new generation airliners like the 737 were also trialed on the old 707 prototype. There was one more important task left for the aircraft when it was fitted with a variation of the ALS for development work in conjunction with the Space Shuttle. On January 22, 1970, the Dash Eighty made its last flight as a test aircraft from the Boeing airfield at Everett, Washington. Later, it was flown for storage in the Arizona desert at Davis-Monthan Air Force Base (AFB). The aircraft had flown 2,350 hours on 1,691 flights and contributed valuable information for a variety of applications from the early 707s through the other Boeing airliners, including the 747, to NASA's recoverable space vehicle.

The historic significance of the aircraft was recognized in 1972, and an agreement was reached, and Boeing donated the Dash Eighty to the Smithsonian Institute for preservation. Ferried to Seattle, the aircraft was refurbished by Boeing employees and appeared at the international aviation fair Transpo '72. Heralded as "one of the twelve most significant aircraft of all time," the Dash Eighty was the star of the show. Following the event, the aircraft was flown back to store in Arizona, as there was nowhere for it to be displayed by the Smithsonian. The desert air is ideal for storage, and the Dash Eighty suffered few side effects, it was kept in good order, and was ferried back in Seattle in 1990. Boeing employees once more restored and repainted the Dash Eighty for it to appear at a number of events in 1991 to commemorate the 75th anniversary of the founding of the Boeing Company. Celebrations over, the aircraft returned to storage before it would make its last flight. After years of planning, the National Air and Space Museum Udvar-Hazy Restoration and Display Center in Washington was ready to receive exhibits, and the Dash Eighty made its final flight over Seattle and then across North America to land at Dulles Airport. The Display Center was opened on December 17, 2003, where among the many historic aircraft, the ancestor of over 14,000 Boeing jetliners is on display, alongside another innovative airliner, the only surviving B307 Stratoliner.

Dash Eighty seen at Boeing Field after being repainted in 1991.

A pleasing photograph of Boeing Dash Eighty N70700 taking off on its first flight on July 15, 1954, with Tex Johnston at the controls.

Chapter 5

Airline Sales and Service

P an Am's order showed confidence in the new airliner and encouraged other airlines to follow. It was important that the US domestic carriers bought the Boeing 707 so that foreign operators would also consider the product. At the time when the Dash Eighty first flew, the only other jet airliner in the world was the de Havilland Comet, and that was in trouble following several accidents.

Three BOAC Boeing 707-436s are seen in this shot outside the airline's hangar at London Airport. They are being made ready for the day's flights.

Production Commences

Armed with firm orders from Pan Am and American Airlines, Boeing was able to start production of the civil variant of the aircraft; the military KC-135 was already in production for the USAF and will be considered later. Production 707s differed from the prototype in many details, notably in size, as noted it was wider and longer with a length 136ft 9in and height 41ft 7in. More powerful engines in the form of Pratt & Whitney JT3Cs of 12,500lb thrust each were chosen. Given the Boeing suffix 707-120, the first commercial airliners were designed primarily for US transcontinental sectors – coast to coast – but were capable of trans-Atlantic operations via a refueling stop in Canada or Scotland.

Boeing's accounting department predicted that only after at least 300 airliners had been sold would it break-even, that was assuming development costs had ended, and the aircraft design stabilized for production and selling. Until then, the 707 would be a drain on finances, but development could not cease; a new wing was required for a longer-range model, and this went into development even while the initial batch of aircraft were on the Renton production lines.

The engineering team of Ed Wells, Jack Steiner, William Hamilton, Ken Holtby and Maynard Pennell was given the task of addressing the fact that the Douglas DC-8 (as yet unflown) had a longer range than the 707-120. They produced the required new designs in six weeks and Boeing was able to announce that the 707-320 "Intercontinental," with a range of 4,200 miles, was more than adequate for a nonstop service on the high-density North Atlantic route. It was also sufficient to bring Asia within

A Pan Am Boeing 707 being prepared for departure in Hawaii. (David Oliver)

nonstop range of Europe. Both American Airlines and Pan Am, which had helped launch the 707-120, placed orders for the 707-320.

Meanwhile, the first Boeing 707-120 was taking shape and was rolled out of the Renton plant, and a few days later, on October 16, 1957, First Lady Mrs. Mamie Eisenhower christened the aircraft *Clipper America* at a ceremony in a hangar at Washington Airport, attended by several hundred invited guests. After ground trials and crew training, the aircraft, registered N707PA, made its first flight on December 20, 1957, from the Boeing field.

Almost immediately, it left on a flight to London with Juan Trippe and guests of Boeing and Pan Am onboard. The airline was keen to showcase its new airliner, and the flight established that the 707 could cross the Atlantic with a passenger load. Back in the US, the orders for the 707 were coming in, with Sabena, Air France, BOAC, Braniff International, TWA and Qantas among the first to sign contracts.

The airliner still needed US FAA certification, and after extensive trials, this was issued on September 18, 1958; the 707 could now legally fly commercial sectors carrying fare-paying passengers. Boeing was still not happy with the wing design, and during the pre-certification trials decided that it could be improved upon. A number of changes were incorporated into the production models that differed from the prototype, one the major changes was the fitting of a Krueger flap along the leading edge between the inner and outer engines on early 707-120 and -320 models. This was tested on the first Pan Am example of the aircraft.

Airline Service

Following the proving flight across the Atlantic, on October 26, 1958, Pan Am put the type into regular service on its New York to Paris and Rome route. On board N711PA *Clipper Mayflower* were 111 passengers and 11 crew; the airliner was furnished with 18 first class and 117 economy class seats. No tourist class seating was provided on any of these early Pan Am Boeings. Although Juan Trippe wanted Pan Am to be the first revenue-earning jet flight on this popular route, he was beaten by two BOAC de Havilland Comet 4s that left London and New York simultaneously on October 4. Comets also beat the US airline by being the first jet airliner to cross the Pacific Ocean. In the months that followed, both airlines vied with each other for passengers keen to experience the smooth and quick jet service. In fact, Rome was not ready for the aircraft, and neither was Le Bourget in Paris. The latter made noise measurements on the proving flights and reluctantly agreed to allow the 707 to land.

The Douglas DC-7C fleet was the pride of Pan Am and was popular with passengers and pilots alike, but when the Boeing 707 arrived that all changed. Trippe may have bought the 707 as a stopgap until the DC-8 became available, but he quickly came to regard the 707 as the aircraft for the premier US overseas airline and advertised it heavily across the world. The 707 could fly nearly twice as fast as the DC-7C, carrying nearly twice the number of passengers. It also did so at a smaller cost per seat mile and, being a turbojet, required fewer hours in the maintenance hangar. Delivery price for each Pan Am 707-120 was about US$6m, when one adds in training, spares and support, but soon after the inaugural trans-Atlantic flight, the aircraft was operating at 100 per cent load factors, helping pay off the purchase price. Juan Trippe ordered more Boeing 707s for the airline.

American Airlines had also received its first examples of the 707 and, on January 25, 1959, operated the first commercial coast-to-coast jet service from Los Angeles to Idlewild, New York. This was flown by N7502 *Flagship Oklahoma*, which flew back the same day with a full load of passengers. American Airlines was the only operator to carry four crew, three being usual, on the flight deck. It added a second officer to handle navigation and communications duties. This was brought about by the lack of understanding by many air traffic controllers in US airspace, who dealt with the fast jet in the same manner as the slower piston engine aircraft. Pilots found that they reached reporting points far too

Libyan Arab Airlines' gleaming Boeing 707-3L5C (5A-DAK) was once the personal aircraft of Colonel Gaddafi.

Qantas ordered a special version of the Boeing 707 for its routes across the Pacific Ocean to Hawaii and Los Angeles.

quickly before they had to switch to the next checkpoint. Hence the additional member of the crew to take over that part of the flight. It was a short-lived role, as air traffic soon came up to speed with the new jets' requirements.

One of the most colorful operators of the 707 was US carrier Braniff Airways, which was among the first to order the airliner, and it received its first example in November 1959. Its aircraft were designated 707-227s and were fitted with Pratt & Whitney JT4A-3 engines with 15,800lb thrust for operations in the hot and high South American destinations served by Braniff. Just five of these models were built, and only Braniff operated the type; it later purchased 707-327Cs and also bought four ex-Qantas 707-138s. Braniff gained fame when, in 1965, it changed its name to Braniff International and painted its aircraft, including the 707s, in various bold colors; the fuselage was in one overall color with the wings, engine nacelles, and tail surfaces in white, a large 'BI' logo was featured on the fin. This use of a strong color was at a time when airliners were mostly sedately painted in liveries, usually red and white or blue and white, that had been established many years previously. Braniff also took the opportunity to redesign and change the interiors of the aircraft, using different fabrics and strong colors to match the exterior tones; new designed crew uniforms were also introduced. However, the bright Boeing 707s did not last long in their new liveries and were sold off 1971, leaving the rest of the Braniff fleet to

An early example of a Pan Am Boeing 707, photographed at London Airport in 1959.

continue on the extensive North and South American route. Problems within the company saw various changes in management and Braniff started to lose its market share; it soldiered on but eventually was overtaken by financial problems and went out of business in 1982.

Special Model

Boeing was keen to sell the 707 to Qantas, which was operating Lockheed Constellations and was under pressure from Britain to buy the Comet. Captain Ritchie, technical manager for Qantas, flew the 707 prototype and was impressed by the way it handled; he was sold but had to convince the Qantas board that it should buy the 707. Douglas was also pitching for the Qantas contact but could not show an operating DC-8; matters dragged even though Boeing offered to take Qantas' piston-engined airliners in part exchange for 707s. Chief executives from the airline, including founder and chairman Sir Hudson Fysh and managing director C. O. Turner, visited both aircraft manufacturers before making their minds up.

Douglas was offering customers two versions of the DC-8: a continental or domestic version and an intercontinental. The main difference being the choice of a smaller engine for the domestic model, Pratt & Whitney J57 with 10,000lb thrust, or the same aircraft with the larger 17,000lb thrust Pratt & Whitney J75 engines. Boeing too was offering two versions for the same applications and Qantas was in a hurry; the DC-8 had yet to fly, whereas the 707 was already flying as a prototype with orders from US airlines as well as the military.

A major requirement for any jet ordered by Qantas was that it could fly the Fiji (Nadi) to Honolulu sector of the Pacific route. This long, overwater distance problem was compounded by the short and humped length of the runway (7,000ft) at Nadi. Qantas put this to the two manufacturers and awaited their comments; Douglas did not want to alter or modify its DC-8 to increase range, but Boeing was far more innovative and came up with a perfect solution. Boeing sold Qantas the special 707-138. This was a standard 707-120, which had six fuselage frames removed, three in front of the wings, and three aft. The frames in the 707 were each 20in apart, this resulted in a shortening of the fuselage by 10ft and reduced seating capacity to 154. Because the maximum take-off weight (247,000lb) remained the same as that of the 707-120, the 707-138 was able to fly the longer routes that Qantas needed; four uprated versions of the JT3C-6 engines, giving 500lb more thrust, were fitted to this variant. Boeing promised delivery of this model for 1959, which meant that Qantas could continue to operate its Super Constellations on the sector without the need for an interim aircraft, such as the Bristol Britannia and Comet 4, which had been considered.

Chief pilot of Pan Am, Richard Vinal, in the left-hand seat of the Dash Eighty during a test flight.

On September 6, 1956, Australian Minister for Civil Aviation Athol Townley announced that government approval had been given for Qantas to purchase seven Boeing 707-138 airliners with delivery beginning in May 1959. Worth £18.8m, the contract made Qantas the first airline in the world outside the US to operate American jet airliners. Work on new buildings and facilities commenced at the Qantas engineering base at Mascot, Sydney Airport, for the arrival of the Boeing 707. The Australian government reluctantly sanctioned funds for the extension of the runways at Sydney Airport to take the new jet. Boeing had the first Qantas 707 (VH-EBA) ready to be towed out of the Seattle plant on February 16, 1959. It made its first flight on March 20, and then had to undergo tests by the FAA to ensure that its handling characteristics had not been affected by the reduction in length. On June 29, Captain Ritchie, Sir Hudson Fysh, Bill Allen, and other guests boarded the aircraft, now named *City of Canberra*, for the delivery flight to Sydney, where they arrived on July 2. The aircraft had taken 16hrs 10mins actual flying time between San Francisco and Sydney; the previous best time for the same sector, by a Pan Am DC-7C, had been 27hrs 30mins. After a few days flying around Australia, VH-EBA left Sydney on July 29 to inaugurate the first Qantas jet service to San Francisco. By this time, there were 41 Boeing 707s in service with American operators and they had logged 30,000 hours in eight months of commercial operations.

Qantas returned its seven aircraft to Boeing to be fitted with the Pratt & Whitney JT3D turbofan engine, which had been certified for use. The aircraft were back in service in 1961 as 707-138Bs and were fitted with other modifications such as a ventral fin, wing fillets, and a fully boosted rudder. Qantas adopted the branding "V-Jet" for its fan-engined 707s; the V was for vannus, the Latin for fan. The first converted aircraft to fly was VH-EBH *City of Darwin* on April 13, 1961. Over the ensuing years, Qantas would operate a total of 35 various 707s, the -138s being converted to all-cargo duties in 1968. No other airline operated the 707-138 version, which remained unique to Qantas. The airline flew its last 707 service on March 25, 1979, when it became an all-747 airline. Several ex-Qantas 707s were sold to other airlines, including Braniff International in the US.

Dawn departure of a Qantas 707-138 from Honolulu on an around the world flight in 1961. (François Prins Collection)

Above: Qantas used its V-Jet fleet of Boeing 707-138s extensively on the Pacific route, as well as within Australia.

Left: BOAC B707-436 being pushed back on the apron outside the airline's maintenance base at London Airport.

These noise suppressors meant that BOAC could test run engines at London Airport at any time of the day.

BOAC Boeing 707 being repositioned outside the maintenance building at London Airport. Note the engine intake covers.

Pan Am Boeing 707 N707PA photographed on a test flight before delivery to the airline in 1958.

World Service

Britain had pioneered jet airline travel with the de Havilland Comet, but the accidents during the early operations had plunged BOAC into despair. It stayed with the Comet and would later operate the type in its developed form but had to also consider the Boeing 707. When the proposed Vickers VC7 airliner was canceled in November 1955, BOAC had no option but to look at the American jet, it had to fight government pressure to buy British and to get access to foreign reserve funds. The UK government agreed but demanded that there had to be a high local content if BOAC was to buy the 707. The airline became the launch customer for the Intercontinental version but specified Rolls-Royce Conway Mk 508 turbofan engines in place of the Pratt & Whitney units for its 707-420s. This was agreed by Boeing, and, in October 1956, a contract was signed for 15 aircraft with delivery in 1958.

UK certification requirements relating to engine-out go-arounds resulted in Boeing increasing the height of the tail fin on all 707 variants, as well as adding a ventral fin beneath the tail cone, which was retrofitted on earlier -120 and -220 aircraft. These modifications also aided in providing better overall stability and were incorporated in production aircraft. The first BOAC aircraft was rolled out on December 12, 1958, and made its first on May 19, 1959. The delay was caused by some additional modifications that were required by the UK Air Registration Board with regard to stability. A full

Certificate of Airworthiness was issued on April 24, 1960, and the Boeing 707-420 entered BOAC service. However, Lufthansa, which had also ordered the Conway-powered version, beat BOAC into service in March 1960, but it returned its examples to Boeing shortly afterwards to have the fin modifications carried out. BOAC's modifications had made a tremendous difference to the handling of the 707 and, as already noted, they were retrofitted to existing aircraft, including the Pan Am fleet.

On May 3, 1960, the first BOAC Boeing 707 (G-APFD) took off on its inaugural flight; this was a proving flight from London Airport to New York via Prestwick and went without incident. The airline used the call-sign "Jet Speedbird 001" for the first time, and this would be in regular use from that time, through the daily Concorde flights to New York and for current all-business class flight from London to New York. BOAC 707s proved popular with passengers, and by August 1960, the airline was operating nine trans-Atlantic flights daily, with Comet 4s and Britannias sharing the load. Comets were gradually withdrawn from the North Atlantic route, with the final flight being made from New York to London on October 16, 1960. Belgian airline Sabena stole a march on BOAC by operating the first scheduled 707 Manchester to New York flight on April 20 that year, and BOAC responded by introducing 707s on the route in October in place of the Britannias that had been operating the service. The year 1960 saw a tremendous increase in air traffic across the Atlantic, and the main carriers were able to reduce their fares significantly; in the case of Pan Am from US$270 to $210. It also introduced a 21-day excursion fare of $300 return, which proved popular and was emulated in due course by BOAC, Air France, Lufthansa, KLM and Sabena.

As the BOAC 707s arrived, they were impressed on various routes and the airline added further examples, including the 707-336 series, which returned better fuel economy over a longer range. The airline purchased the convertible cargo/passenger (336C) and the all-passenger (336B) versions, and they were the first BOAC aircraft to be fitted with in-flight entertainment systems. BOAC operated some 30 examples of the 707, many of which then went on to serve with British Airways (BA) on its formation in 1974 and, with the arrival of the Boeing 747, carried on until the 1980s, mainly to the popular holiday destinations. The 707-336C was used largely in the cargo role by the end of its time with the airline. Several ex-BOAC/BA 707s were bought by British European Airways (BEA) for use on its longer routes.

The 707 quickly became the most popular jetliner of its time and its popularity led to rapid developments in airport terminals, runways, airline catering, baggage handling, reservations systems, and other air transport infrastructure. The pace of piston-engined airliners meant that air travel was more leisurely and also the domain of the business or government traveler, or the financially better-off. The Boeing 707 and the DC-8 changed all that: they were faster and cheaper to operate; jets required less time in the maintenance hangar and offered more flying hours, fares came down and with it the increase in passenger numbers. Airports had to change almost every aspect of their operation, including the upgrading of air traffic control systems to cope with the extra traffic and the higher operating speeds. For example, separation distances between landings had to be increased.

By the mid-1960s, almost all the major world airlines were operating the Boeing 707 in one version or another. Air India International and El Al Israeli Airline both ordered the Rolls-Royce Conway-powered 707. The Indian carrier established a record time for flying from Seattle to Bombay via New York and London on its delivery flight February 21, 1960. It began scheduled operations to London on April 19 and New York on May 14; the Bombay–Tokyo service with 707s commenced in January the following year. Air India had operated Lockheed Constellations on these routes, and the arrival of the 707 made a difference, not only to time saving, but also to operating costs per passenger mile. Encouraged by the success of the first six 707s, the airline ordered further examples, including the 707-337 long-range, some of which were later converted to the freighter role. When the 747 was

British Airtours 707 in the new British Airways livery; the airline's 707s were powered by Rolls-Royce Conway engines.

Chinese state airlines operated several examples of the Boeing 707 on overseas and internal routes for many years.

launched, Air India was one of the first to place an order and as the 747 delivered, the 707 was retired, many sold off to smaller airlines; the final Air India 707 passenger service was flown from Harare to Delhi on October 29, 1986.

Middle East Airlines (MEA) had originally ordered the DC-8, but when the Lebanon Intra Bank, which held 65 per cent of MEA's shares, collapsed in 1966, Douglas canceled the contract. With some cash injected from other sources, MEA was able to continue trading, and in August 1968, ordered four Boeing 707-320Cs, with the first aircraft being delivered in November that year. The aircraft (OD-AFC) had hardly entered service with MEA when it was destroyed on the ground at Beirut Airport on December 28, by Israeli commandos in retaliation for an attack on Israeli passengers at Athens Airport. MEA lost various other 707s in the troubles that besieged Lebanon in the years that followed. The airline left Lebanon and operated out of Paris on charter and cargo flights, as well as a reduced passenger schedule to Africa and to some Middle East destinations. MEA was able to move back to Beirut eventually, but the 707 series had reached the end of their lives and were finally retired in 1995.

Closing Stages

The exponential growth in air travel led to the 707 being a victim of its own success; it became too small to handle the increased passenger densities on the routes for which it was designed. The 707-320 could be configured to carry up to 219 passengers but not in great comfort; Douglas managed to stretch its DC-8 to fit 269 seats but a larger airliner was clearly required. Stretching the fuselage was not a viable option because the installation of larger, more powerful engines would in turn need a larger undercarriage, which was not feasible given the design's limited ground clearance. Boeing's answer to the problem was the first twin-aisle airliner – the Boeing 747.

The 707's first-generation engine technology was also rapidly becoming obsolete in the areas of noise and fuel economy, especially after the 1973 oil crisis. Most of the airlines that had bought the jet airliner new from Boeing were starting to wind operations down and sell off their fleets. There was no shortage of takers for this most capable of aircraft, and soon several charter operators in the US and Europe bought secondhand 707s to replace piston engine or first-generation turboprop aircraft. In the

UK, British Caledonian, Cunard-Eagle, Monarch and Dan-Air were among the first to put the 707 into service on their routes.

By the 1970s, the Boeing 707 was being replaced by the Boeing 747 with the major airlines, but there was still life in the 707, and, as noted, they went on to serve with smaller carriers. They also found a new lease of life in the cargo world, with the convertible example being highly sought after and the earlier passenger types being converted to carry cargo. Prices were not high, and when the lower operating costs were included, the 707 was an attractive option. Spares were plentiful, and after 20 years of service there were many aeronautical engineering companies that were certified to work on the 707.

From records we know that the last Western operation by a 707 was by TWA, which flew the last scheduled 707 flight for passengers by a US carrier on October 30, 1983. The airliner was still a familiar sight at many airports around the world and was given an extended lease of life when its noisy engines were fitted with a hush-kit developed by Shannon Engineering in Seattle. Known as the "Quiet 707," the system was retrofitted to many 707s that had been grounded due to the noise regulations. Boeing is on record as saying that, by 1989, more 707s were in service than before the hush-kit was available.

In 2007, LADE of Argentina retired its 707-320Bs from regular passenger service and Saha Airlines of Iran stopped operating its two 707s on a scheduled passenger service in 2013. Boeing built a long-lasting aircraft that opened up air travel for many and can be still be found flying nearly 60 years after the Dash Eighty made its first flight.

Two BOAC 707-436s at London Airport being readied for the day's schedules.

Chapter 6

Military Service

Late in 1943, the USAAF invited five American aircraft manufacturers, Boeing, Convair, North American Aviation, Northrop, and Martin, to submit designs for the first American jet bomber. By November the following year, prototypes had been commissioned from each of the manufacturers for a bomber that could fly at 500mph at an operating altitude of between 35,000 and 40,000ft. By the end of World War Two, all five had produced designs of a conventional-looking bomber with straight wings, no propellers and with four jet engines attached in place of piston engines. Only the Martin XB-48 was slightly different; it had its main undercarriage located on the centerline, which retracted directly into the fuselage. This kept the much thinner wing clear of undercarriage wheel wells. The other designs had opted for a standard tricycle undercarriage. Boeing was under pressure to come up with a design that would follow naturally from the B-17 Flying Fortress and B-29 Superfortress aircraft that had contributed to the recent war and made Boeing a byword for bombers.

Aerodynamicist George Schairer was keen to use a swept back wing, but if he did so then time would not be on Boeing's side, as it would take much longer to design and test in a wind tunnel before a prototype could be built. Project manager Ed Wells believed in what Schairer was trying to do and took the matter to Bill Allen, who had just taken over as president of Boeing. Allen was impressed and gave the word to proceed; within a week a wing with a sweep of 30 degrees had been built and was ready to be tested in the wind tunnel. The original straight wing Boeing XB-47 design showed the jet engines buried in the wing roots, but with a swept wing this was not possible, so they were housed in pods attached to pylons under the wing. After various trials using the wing to discover the optimum position for the engines, now increased to six, they were separated into four pods; two carried twin engines mounted close inboard and two with a single engine in each mounted further out towards the

NATO-operated Boeing E-3A Sentry has been a great success supporting the organization's operations around the globe. (Cliff Knox)

Gleaming in the sun on its delivery flight is a Boeing C-135 of the USAF MATS.

wingtips. Work proceeded, and by September 1947, the XB-47 was ready to be rolled out of the plant for ground checks; the first flight was made on December 17. The other contenders had already flown their designs, but only the North American Aviation B-45 and the Boeing B-47 earned production contracts, and the B-47 would ultimately be produced in far larger numbers than any other American jet bomber. Boeing's gamble had paid off.

Air Force Transport

With the experience gained from the B-47 Stratojet, Boeing was in an advantageous position to use the data for other applications. The company wanted to build an airliner to rival the Comet, but US airlines were reluctant to consider a change from the proven Douglas and Lockheed piston-engined airliners. Boeing knew that one way of enticing the airlines would be to address the USAF requirement for an aerial tanker to resupply the fast jet bombers mentioned above and the new generation of jet fighters then coming into service.

In 1954, USAF's SAC held a competition for a jet-powered aerial refueling tanker. Lockheed's tanker version of the proposed Lockheed L-193 airliner with tail-mounted engines was declared the winner in 1955. However, as the Boeing proposal was already flying, its military Dash Eighty, the KC-135, could be delivered two years earlier and a small order for 29 tankers was placed, but within a few weeks, Air Force Secretary Harold Talbott ordered 250 KC-135 tankers until the Lockheed's design could be manufactured. This never happened, and SAC dropped the idea rather than support two tanker designs. Between 1955 and 1964, the USAF ordered 820 KC-135A Stratotankers and its variants.

The USAF ordered the type in its original guise, that is before the aircraft was made wider as an airliner. Known as the 717 within the company and as the KC-135 Stratotanker by the Air Force, it was quite different from the commercial airliner. The 717 was shorter and narrower than the 707 with only about 20 per cent shared components. A penalty clause was inserted into the contract where Boeing would have to pay the Pentagon if any tooling paid for by the Air Force was used to extend or enhance the commercial 707. Both types were developed alongside each other, and at first, the 717 was its own type quite unlike the 707. The initial KC-135 flew on August 31, 1956, and was delivered to Castle AFB in California in June the following year.

The first KC-135 takes shape alongside production C-97 Stratofreighters destined for the USAF.

The Boeing RC-135V Rivet Jet is one of the most efficient surveillance aircraft. (USAF/DoD)

The Boeing KC-135 is one of the most versatile platforms and has entered service with several armed forces as a tanker/transporter.

A pleasing photo of a Strategic Air Command (SAC) KC-135 on a delivery flight as it gets close to the camera aircraft.

Tanker and Variants

The success of the KC-135 led to it being used for a number of applications, along with the 707 airframe, the US armed forces have adapted and utilized the aircraft in all manner of guises. As the lead design, the KC-135 was built in large numbers and has been in military service with several countries for many years.

The basic KC-135A carries 31,200 US gallons of fuel in tanks extending from tip to tip in the wing, along the lower portion of the fuselage and in a tank above the floor at the tail. Almost all the fuel can be transferred via a Boeing pivoted Flying Boom under the rear fuselage, which can be lowered down and "flown" by powered control surfaces by the boom operator lying in the rear fuselage. Some KC-135s have been fitted with the UK-built FLR Mk 32B refueling pods at the wing tips; this enables the refueling of US Navy, US Marine Corps and most NATO tactical jet aircraft while keeping the tail-mounted refueling boom. The tanker can refuel two receivers at the same time, which increases throughput compared with the boom drogue adapter.

The USAF made great use of the KC-135 fleet to support the B-47 and B-52 bombers that were always airborne during the Cold War years, when the Soviet Union and the US continually rattled sabers at each other. Tankers were much in demand during the Vietnam War and Boeing received further orders for the type. Keeping pace with utilization meant that variants were identified, and the 707 platform was adapted for a variety of roles. The most numerous of the extended family must be the EC-135, most of which are airborne command posts, although some are radio platforms and the EC-135N series are spacecraft trackers.

The EC-135 aircraft were part of the "Looking Glass" program from the Cold War years, although it is still active and operating in a much-modified form. US nuclear strategy depends on its ability to command, control, and communicate with its nuclear forces under all conditions. Looking Glass is an essential element of that ability, the crew and staff ensure there is always an aircraft ready to direct bombers and missiles from the air should ground-based command centers be destroyed or rendered inoperable. Looking Glass is intended to guarantee that US strategic forces will act only in the manner dictated by the president. It took the name Looking Glass because the mission mirrored ground-based command, control, and communications. EC-135 aircraft carry a crew of at least 15, including at least one or more general officer. SAC began the Looking Glass mission on February 3, 1961, and Looking Glass aircraft were continuously airborne 24 hours a day for over 29 years, accumulating more than 281,000 accident-free flying hours. On July 24, 1990, continuous airborne surveillance ceased, but remained on ground or airborne alert 24 hours a day.

Allied to this program and in support of the US Test Readiness Program that was initiated in response to the Limited Test Ban Treaty of 1963, Sandia National Laboratories configured three NC-135 aircraft as flying laboratories to support atmospheric testing of nuclear weapons, should testing have resumed. These aircraft were based at Kirtland AFB. Work was initiated in 1963 and the aircraft remained in service with Sandia until 1976, flying principally for Sandia, the Los Alamos National Laboratory, and the Lawrence Livermore National Laboratory. The Atomic Energy Commission (AEC) maintained controlling oversight of the NC-135 flight test aircraft. After 1976, the aircraft flew for the Air Force Laboratory in a similar role. Most recently, NC-135 aircraft monitored the North Korean nuclear tests that were carried out in January 2013.

While flying simulations for the Test Readiness Program, the science teams assigned to the NC-135 aircraft realized that their flying laboratories could be effectively used to study solar eclipses, cosmic rays entering the atmosphere and the effects of magnetic fields in the ionosphere. Program scientists petitioned the AEC to allow the use of the aircraft for such scientific research. The petition was approved, and research continued through 1975. Several missions have been flown during eclipses, providing valuable scientific data, which also assisted in the development of avionic equipment for other applications.

Another important variant is the Boeing RC-135, which is a reconnaissance aircraft used by the USAF to support theater and national level intelligence consumers with near real-time on-scene collection, analysis, and dissemination capabilities. Based on the C-135 Stratolifter airframe, various types of RC-135s have been in service since 1961. Because the RC-135A and RC-135B series, with their large, nose-mounted radomes, were so different internally and electronically, they were developed by Boeing as the Model 739 rather than as 717 variants. As they were modified by the military over the ensuing years to take different equipment, they were given various other suffixes.

The first RC-135 variant, the RC-135A, was ordered in 1962 by the USAF to replace the Boeing RB-50 Superfortress. Originally nine were ordered, but this was later reduced to four. Boeing allocated the variant the designation Boeing 739-700, but they were a modified variant of the KC-135A then in production. They used the same J57-P engines of the tanker variant but carried cameras in a housing just aft of the nose undercarriage bay where the forward fuel tank was normally located. They had no refueling system fitted, and they were used for photographic and surveying tasks.

The next variant ordered was the RC-135B for use as an ELINT aircraft to replace the Boeing RB-47H Stratojet on ELINT duties. Similar to the earlier variants the RC-135Bs were fitted with TF-33 turbofans rather than the older J57s. These ten aircraft were delivered directly into storage in 1965,

The boom operator's view from a KC-135 Stratotanker of a Boeing B-52 Stratofortress as it comes in for fuel.

while they awaited fitment of an improved electronics suite. By 1967, they had emerged as RC-135Cs and were all delivered that year. The refueling boom was not fitted and the boom operator's station was used as a camera bay, for a KA-59 camera. Externally, the aircraft were also fitted with sideways looking airborne radar (SLAR) antenna on the lower forward fuselage. The RC-135Bs were the last of the new aircraft to be built, all the RC variants that followed were modified aircraft, either from earlier RC variants or from tankers.

Initially employed by SAC for reconnaissance, the RC-135 fleet has also participated in every armed conflict involving US assets during its service life. From Vietnam to operation *Desert Shield, Desert Storm, Enduring Freedom,* and *Iraqi Freedom,* the RC-135 has been on duty operating in all weather conditions. When not required in theater, the RC-135 fleet is based at Offutt AFB, Nebraska, and operated by 55th Wing, using forward operating bases worldwide as required. 55th Wing operates 22 platforms in three variants: three RC-135S Cobra Balls, two RC-135U Combat Sents, and 17 RC-135V/W Rivet Joints. The last has been given a new lease of life for use by the RAF.

Rivet Joint aircraft have flown over 8,000 combat missions, including operations over Afghanistan and elsewhere. With the cancellation of the Nimrod MRA.4 and the retirement of the Nimrod R.1, the UK had to turn to the US, and in March 2010, the Ministry of Defence reached an agreement with the US government to purchase three RC-135W Rivet Joint aircraft along with associated ground systems. The aircraft were being totally rebuilt from old airframes.

A Boeing EC-18B with the large nose radome that characterizes the model. Inside is a moving radar scanner to track missiles and space vehicles.

A SAC Boeing KC-135A with boom extended waits for the receiver aircraft to close in and connect for fuel transfer.

On the ground attracting attention are a KC-135 and C-97, while the Dash Eighty flies overhead leading the YB-52 Stratofortress.

New Engines

All KC-135s were originally equipped with Pratt & Whitney J57-P-59W turbojet engines, which produced 10,000lb of thrust dry, and approximately 13,000lb of thrust wet. The latter is achieved through the use of water injection on take-off. Some 670 US gallons of water are injected into the engines over the course of two and a half minutes. This water enables a second set of fuel injectors to activate without melting the turbine buckets. The water turns to steam and is ejected out the rear of the engine, increasing the exhaust mass and increasing thrust. The engine runs somewhat hotter, with more engine noise but has the desired effect. However, in the ensuing years, the noise levels became prohibitive, and more fuel-efficient engines that had become available were sought. Boeing was already retrofitting airliners with turbofan engines and the USAF was offered a similar modification.

During the 1980s, the first modification program saw 157 Air Force Reserve and Air National Guard (ANG) tankers fitted with Pratt & Whitney TF33-PW-102 engines from 707 airliners that had been retired in the late 1970s and early 1980s. The re-engined tanker, designated the KC-135E, was 14 per cent more fuel efficient than the KC-135A and could offload 20 per cent more fuel on long duration flights. The KC-135E fleet has since either been re-engined into the R-model configuration or placed into long term storage, as Congress has prevented the Air Force from formally retiring them. This program added 17 KC-135B Stratotankers, 30 C-135B Stratolifters, ten RC-135Bs, five EC-135Cs, and five VC-135B staff transports. The French Air Force also ordered 12 TF-33-powered KC-135B tankers at the same time.

The second modification program re-engined 500 aircraft with new CFM International CFM56 (military designation F108) engines produced by General Electric and Snecma. The CFM-56 turbofans are capable of producing approximately 22,500lb of thrust, nearly a 100 per cent increase in thrust compared with the original J57 engines. The re-engined tanker, designated either the KC-135R or KC-135T, can offload up to 50 per cent more fuel. The KC-135R's operational range is 60 per cent greater than the KC-135E for comparable fuel offloads, providing a wider range of basing options.

WC-135B Constant Phoenix atmospheric collection aircraft is used to collect samples from the atmosphere for the purpose of detecting and identifying nuclear explosions. (Cliff Knox)

An RAF Boeing E-3D AEW 1 Sentry seen near its base at RAF Waddington, where the type is operated by 8 Squadron. (François Prins)

Flaps down and trailing its refueling boom, a KC-135R Stratotanker makes a slow pass at Royal International Air Tattoo (RIAT) in 2005. (Cliff Knox)

The aircraft was 25 per cent more fuel efficient, cost 25 per cent less to operate and was 96 per cent quieter than the KC-135A; sideline noise levels at takeoff were reduced from 126 to 99 decibels.

There are too many variations of the KC-135 series to list, but they have been used for many roles from those listed above to one-off missions and in support of NASA space programs. Engine manufacturers have trialed new powerplants on the airframe with the cooperation of the USAF. One major modification that was made was or the role of Airborne Warning and Control Systems (AWACS). This was born out of an Air Force requirement for early warning of Soviet aircraft and missiles flying high or low towards US air space.

Sentry AWACS

To address a new USAF requirement, a commercial Boeing 707-320B airliner was acquired by the manufacturer and converted to carry an above-fuselage rotating radome, or rotodome, housing a long-range surveillance radar suite. The AWACS radar is capable of tracking aircraft over both land and water at any altitude; the surveillance radar is coupled to extensive on-board avionics equipment that enables the mission crew to relay early warning of hostile air operations and to coordinate the response of friendly forces. Mission endurance is around 10hrs or 5,000 miles, although this can be extended by aerial refueling, On the RAF version, known as the Boeing E-3D Sentry AEW 1, the crew complement of 18 comprises four flight-deck crew, three technicians and an 11-person mission crew. The mission crew comprises a tactical director (mission crew commander), a fighter allocator, three weapons controllers, a surveillance controller, two surveillance operators, a data-ink manager, a communications operator, and an electronic support measures operator.

Fitted with Northrop-Grumman AN/APY-2 high-performance, multi-mode look-down radar, the Sentry's roles include air and sea surveillance, airborne command and control, weapons control, and use as an extensive communications platform. It is a highly capable and effective platform, capable of detecting submarines and surface craft as well as aircraft in the role it was originally designed for. Since it first entered service with the USAF in 1977, the E-3 has been continually upgraded as better radar and other electronic equipment has been developed. Sentry aircraft from the USAF were used in 1982 to scan the skies over the British Task Force as it steamed towards the Falkland Islands. For its part, the Argentine Air Force made extensive use of civilian 707s for long-range maritime patrols; these were not dedicated surveillance aircraft, but they did try and get close to the British forces to monitor the situation. On occasion, the 707s were spotted and escorted away by Royal Navy Sea Harriers and once a Nimrod MR2 arrived alongside to encourage the Argentine crew to leave the area. This lack of a dedicated intelligence platform may have been addressed by the arrival of a RC-707 converted in Israel a few years ago.

Military Transport

After Boeing had delivered several hundred KC-135s to SAC, the military interest in the program broadened when, in 1961, the aircraft was ordered by the USAF's MATS for a modern passenger/cargo jet transport. Boeing had already produced design brochures for such an aircraft, which was ordered for MATS as the C-135 Stratolifter. This model was almost identical to the KC-135A but with a larger fin and without the Stratotanker's refueling capability.

Since the first C-135 was built in August 1956, it has been a visible fixture of the USAF. Although the majority of the 820 units were developed as KC-135A Stratotankers, they have also performed numerous transport and special-duty functions. Forty-five aircraft were built as C-135A or C-135B transports with the tanking equipment excluded. Fifteen C-135As were built, powered by Pratt & Whitney J57 turbojets, for use in the cargo/transport role to carry 126 passengers. Some were also

A Boeing KC-135H Stratotanker with boom and hoses folded away to keep the airflow clean makes a low pass for the camera. (Cliff Knox)

used in the VIP role for government and high-ranking military personnel. Later, almost all C-135As were upgraded with Pratt & Whitney TF33 turbofan engines and wide-span tailplanes and were redesignated C-135E. Later on, most of the C-135Es were re-engined again, using the more powerful turbofan engine, the CFM International F108 (CFM56).

The C-135 transports were also used for various other military applications along similar lines as the KC-135s. In some cases, just one or two aircraft were modified for a different role, and when that program had ended, they would revert to their original configuration. For instance, the C-135C communications aircraft serves as an aerial test bed for emerging technologies. Developmental tests using this aircraft have demonstrated the capability to fly precision approaches using a local area differential GPS system. This modified C-135 has been fitted with a millimeter wave camera and a radome to test the camera's generation of video images of the forward scene in low-visibility conditions. The aircraft, which in the VIP/Distinguished Visitor transport role seats 14 passengers, also gives a Joint Forces Air Component Commander (JFACC) a limited ability to plan and control the simulated battle while in the air en route to the crisis area.

Having been in service since 1956, the KC135 and C-135 and their many variants show no sign of leaving the military scene. In February 2011, the USAF selected the Boeing 767 airliner design to be revised and converted as a tanker with the designation KC-46. Other armed forces using the KC-135 have no plans to replace the aircraft in the near future, and the E-3 Sentry and RC-135 Rivet Joint have continued to be in service into the 2020s, some 70 years since the first flight of the Dash Eighty in 1954.

NATO was the first organization to operate the E-3 Sentry after the USAF had chosen the type for service.

Other books you might like:

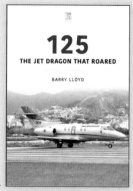

Historic Commercial Aircraft
Series, Vol. 11

Historic Commercial Aircraft
Series, Vol. 10

Historic Commercial Aircraft
Series, Vol. 9

Historic Commercial Aircraft
Series, Vol. 8

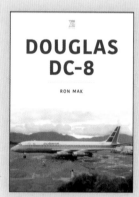

Historic Commercial Aircraft
Series, Vol. 7

Historic Commercial
Aircraft Series, Vol. 2

For our full range of titles please visit:
shop.keypublishing.com/books